The Black Arch

DOCTOR WHO
(1996)

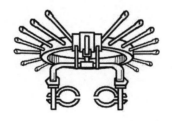

By Paul Driscoll

Published November 2018 by Obverse Books

Cover Design © Cody Schell

Text © Paul Driscoll, 2018

Range Editors: Philip Purser-Hallard, Paul Simpson

Paul would like to thank:

Matthew Jacobs for his generosity in contributing to this volume. JR Southall for putting the two of us in touch. Kara Dennison for her unique insights and recollections from a US perspective. All those who took the time to participate in the survey and/or sent me their own reflections. Philip Purser-Hallard for his patience, diligence and invaluable advice. Jenny and the children for letting me open my laptop, even at the most inconvenient of times.

For Dennis and Hilda, George and Ivy

Also Available

CONTENTS

Foreword

by Matthew Jacobs

I sincerely believe the eighth Doctor would adore this book.

As the eighth Doctor says in my 1996 TV movie screenplay, 'I love humans. They always see patterns in things that aren't there.' That is a statement that came from my heart too, not just the character. It is honest and warm, and I believe fans have responded to that sincerity over the years. Indeed, the eighth Doctor's sincerity is one of the reasons why, with only one TV outing, Paul McGann's Doctor stayed alive and kicking for 17 years on radio and in novels.

The eighth Doctor lasted longer than any other Doctor, existing in his own dimension until they finally had to kill him in 2013 so he could regenerate into the War Doctor. He celebrates the best in people, and the very human ability to analyse its environment to a fanatical level is what has made us into the strange, wonderful and (sometimes) frightening species that we are. This ability fuels scientists and artists alike, it elevates us, and the Doctor celebrates us.

Paul Driscoll has definitely seen all the patterns there are to see in our production of *Doctor Who* (the TV movie that we made for Fox, Universal and the BBC back in 1996). I have read every page of this book. It only took a short day. It's well written and moves quickly. I am compelled and intrigued by patterns Paul can see that were never intended, and delighted by the patterns he has seen that so few people have ever spotted that were absolutely intended.

Intended or not, his observations are always valid and entertaining. This is without doubt the most thorough and complete analysis of the TV Movie I have ever read – and there have been quite a few. If I had any idea what I was writing back in 1995-6 was going to be analysed this deeply, I might never have started!

Where Paul Driscoll hits the nail on the head are in sections like 'A Tale of Two Operas' where he goes beyond simply charting how I wanted to use Turandot's search for identity as a subtext for a newer romantic and more human vision of the Doctor, but explores how *Madame Butterfly* (the cheaper opera we were finally forced to use) also embraces a subtext that supports the new incarnation of the Doctor. If there was a PhD to be given in **Doctor Who** (and there might be somewhere in America) Paul has certainly earned it.

In 2013 when the eighth Doctor was brought back for the web-episode entitled 'The Night of the Doctor' I was reluctantly drawn back into the world of fan conventions by Vanessa Yuille who wanted to join forces with me to make a documentary film about going back into a world that I thought hated my work. I was so wrong about the world hating me. Yes, the fans have never forgiven the half-human thing and were traumatised at the time by a Doctor who kissed, but I slowly began to realise that American **Doctor Who** fans are the warmest bunch of humans you might find on this planet. It has been a wild ride, where at the end of the day we realised it's not about the show at all, it's about the community the fans have built. A community I have finally become a part of.

Doctor Who is quintessentially British but for a while there, back in 1996, it was the American fandom and American studios that were fighting to keep him alive. British fans should never forget that. The now millions of **Doctor Who** fans in America and around the world will never let this character die.

But this is the book to end all books on the 1996 TV movie... I hope!

OVERVIEW

Title: *Doctor Who*

Writer: Matthew Jacobs

Director: Geoffrey Sax

Original UK Transmission Dates: 27 May 1996[1]

Running Time: 85m 47s

UK Viewing Figures: 9.08 million

Regular Cast: Paul McGann (The Doctor), Sylvester McCoy (The Old Doctor)

Guest Cast: Eric Roberts (The Master / Bruce), Daphne Ashbrook (Dr Grace Holloway), Yee Jee Tso (Chang Lee), John Novak (Salinger), Michael David Simms (Dr Swift), Catherine Lough (Wheeler), Dolores Drake (Curtis), William Sasso (Pete), Jeremy Radick (Gareth), Eliza Roberts (Miranda), Bill Croft (Motorcycle Policeman), David Hurtubise (Professor Wagg), Joel Wirkkunen (Ted), Dee Jay Jackson (Security Guard), Gordon Tipple (The Old Master), Mi-Jung Lee (News Anchor), Joanna Pyros (News Anchor)

Antagonist: The Master

Novelisation: *Doctor Who: The Novel of the Film* by Gary Russell

Responses:

'This new movie does for **Doctor Who** what Tim Burton's first

---

[1] This followed the first broadcasts in Canada and the USA, on 12 and 14 May respectively.

Batman film did for that formerly silly franchise. It darkens and deepens it, and, quite appropriately, gives it new life.'

[David Bianculli, 'Fox Flick a Who's "Who" of Sci-Fi' *Daily News*, 14 May 1996]

'I'm glad to have **Doctor Who** back, but, though promising, this regeneration hasn't taken yet. There's still extraneous American DNA floating around the matrix, perhaps left there by the Master. It needs to be purged if the Doctor's career is to extend into the new millennium.'

[Kim Newman, 'Doctor Who Has Been Exterminated', *The Independent*, 29 May 1996]

SYNOPSIS

Having exhausted all his regenerations, **the Master** is tried and executed by the Daleks. He entrusts **the Doctor**, still in his seventh life, to return his remains to Gallifrey. However, the remains are still active and escape their casket, creating a timing malfunction in the TARDIS, which effects an emergency landing.

It appears in San Francisco, late on 30 December 1999, with an ambush in progress between rival gangs. Its arrival protects one of them, **Chang Lee**, from gunfire, but the Doctor is shot as he steps outside. Lee calls an ambulance and accompanies the unconscious Doctor to hospital, while the gelatinous snake holding the Master's essence stows away in **Bruce** the paramedic's jacket. The Doctor's accelerated heart rate leads **Dr Salinger** to call in cardiologist **Grace Holloway** from her date at the opera. None of the medics believe the x-ray evidence that their patient has two hearts, and their confusion during surgery kills the Doctor. When Grace tells Lee his 'friend' is dead, he runs away with his belongings, including the TARDIS key.

Later in the morgue, the Doctor regenerates into his eighth body and escapes, traumatising the attendant **Pete**. Meanwhile Bruce's sleeping body is possessed by the Master.

The next day, New Year's Eve, Grace investigates her deceased patient. With the body apparently stolen, her boss, **Swift**, tries to cover up the evidence of error by destroying the Doctor's x-rays. Grace resigns in protest. As she is leaving she is accosted by the new Doctor, who persuades her of his identity by extracting her surgical probe from his chest. She takes him home, where she finds that her boyfriend has left her after she abandoned him at the opera. The Doctor is disoriented and unsure who he is, though he remembers meeting Puccini – a favourite composer of Grace's – and somehow knows that Grace entered medicine because as a child she hoped to hold back death.

After killing Bruce's wife **Miranda**, the Master returns to the hospital in search of the Doctor. Learning from nurse **Curtis** that the body has disappeared, he seeks out Lee, who he finds inside the TARDIS. Bruce's body is already failing, and the Master persuades Lee that the Doctor has stolen the body that is his by right. He bribes Lee with the Doctor's stash of gold dust to help him 'get it back'. Realising that the TARDIS is granting Lee access to its interior, the Master uses him to open the power source in the cloister room, the Eye of Harmony. This creates a link with the Doctor, abruptly reminding the latter of who he is; it also reveals to the Master that the Doctor himself is half-human. The Master and Lee are able to listen in as the Doctor insists to Grace that the open Eye will destroy the Earth at midnight unless it is closed. To shut it he will need to repair the TARDIS' timing malfunction using the chip from a state-of-the-art atomic clock. Coincidentally one of these is to be unveiled during a New Year's Eve party at the San Francisco Institute of Technological Advancement and Research. Grace, now certain that the Doctor is insane, calls for an ambulance and the Master and Lee answer the summons.

In the vehicle the Doctor spots the Master's snake-like eyes and unmasks him, whereupon he spits venom over Grace. The Doctor and Grace flee but are stopped by a policeman. The Doctor steals his gun and threatens suicide unless he lets them go, but Grace – now convinced that the Doctor is 'the right guy' for her – uses it instead to steal his motorbike. The Master and Lee pursue them to the Institute. The Doctor distracts the atomic clock's creator, **Professor Wagg**, by claiming to be half-human on his mother's side, while at the same time purloining his key card. He steals the chip from the clock and suborns a young security guard, **Gareth**, by giving him a tip to help him pass his exams and become a prominent seismologist. Chased by the Master and the police, they return to the TARDIS, where the Doctor fixes the malfunction and closes the Eye.

He then realises that they are too late – to avert the Earth's destruction now, they must travel back in time to before the TARDIS arrived. Grace has been corrupted by the Master's venom, and knocks the Doctor out. The Master and Lee arrive, and arrange the mirrors mounted around the Eye to enable the Master to steal the Doctor's remaining lives. The Master lets slip that he has 'wasted all his lives' fighting the Doctor, and Lee realises that he has been lied to. He refuses to reopen the Eye, and the Master kills him. Since the Eye only responds to a living, fully human eye – not the dead Lee's, the half-human Doctor's, the Master's or the possessed Grace's – the Master can only open it by relieving Grace of his control. As he begins draining the Doctor's life force, Grace runs to the console room and tries to send the TARDIS back in time; instead it enters a 'temporal orbit' as the Earth is apparently destroyed. Grace helps free the Doctor before the Master kills her too. The Time Lords fight until the Master falls into the Eye and is apparently consumed.

During the temporal orbit, energy from the Eye restores Grace and Lee to life. The Doctor returns the TARDIS to 29 December, apparently undoing the destruction of the Earth, and then to the final moments of New Year's Eve. He lets Lee keep his gold, but warns him to stay away from San Francisco during Christmas 2000. Realising that they each prefer to live their own lives, the Doctor and Grace kiss goodbye beneath the celebratory New Year fireworks.

NOTE ON TERMINOLOGY

The 1996 **Doctor Who** television movie starring Paul McGann has no agreed title beyond that which appears onscreen: *Doctor Who*. Standard **Black Archive** house style, as applied on the cover of this book, is to refer to it by this title, but to add the date to avoid confusion: '*Doctor Who* (1996)'.

In an entire book devoted to the story this would become tedious. Omitting the date, however, would require the reader continually to distinguish between **Doctor Who** the series and *Doctor Who* the story by typography alone. So, for this volume only, we will refer to this story as '*The Movie*', the title given on the cover of both its BBC DVD releases.

ANXIOUS VOICES IN THE WILDERNESS

More has been written about the background and production of *The Movie* (1996) than any other **Doctor Who** story. The fascinating tale of how Philip Segal finally fulfilled his ambition to bring **Doctor Who** back to the screen was even made the subject of a standalone coffee-table book, *Doctor Who: Regeneration* (2000)[2]. The convoluted script-to-screen process began several years before writer Matthew Jacobs was commissioned, with the writer's brief made up of elements and correctives from abandoned proposals. In between Segal's frank recollections of his quest to revive the series, *Regeneration* is generously supplemented by transcripts and summaries of various story proposals, including John Leekley's notorious 'bible' and origin story. They all shed fascinating light on what might have been.

Another book on *The Movie* might then seem unnecessary – after all what can be said that hasn't already been extensively covered? Quite a lot, as it happens. The final script itself has been all-too-easily dismissed or trivialised by commentators, with the performances of its leads, the behind-the-scenes shenanigans and the question of why Fox did not pick up the option for a new series tending to dominate the discussion.

The primary goal of the **Black Archive** range is to focus on the final product, interpreting and analysing structure and meaning in order to arrive at insights that go beyond a straightforward review. In the case of *The Movie*, the wealth of background materials should not be simply ignored, but nor should they be treated as sources for

---

[2] Segal, Philip, with Gary Russell, *Doctor Who: Regeneration*.

writing a production history. Our interest is in what they offer by way of a context for understanding certain aspects of the script and its on-screen realisation. *The Movie* both reflects and responds to a number of commercial, social and political pressures that were prevalent in the mid-1990s. Some are specific to the project itself, to the personalities and stakeholders involved and to the whole debate about how to successfully resurrect one of the BBC's most recognisable series. Others are more existential influences, from popular movies, TV shows and storytelling conventions of the time to anxieties around globalisation and the turn of the millennium.

Popular Perceptions of Doctor Who at the Time

> '**Doctor Who** will be back but not in the near future. When it returns, the programme will be vibrant, vital and improved – not a tired old Time Lord who comes back too soon.'
>
> [BBC statement][3]

This was one of several fan appeasing statements issued by the BBC between 1989 and 1996. Reflective of the BBC's attitude towards the show at the time, it is an astonishingly disparaging statement about what was still one of the corporation's most marketable products. The popular belief that **Doctor Who** had outstayed its welcome and run out of ideas was one that the BBC would continue to propagate even after *The Movie* had aired[4]. On the flip side, the respect for 1960s and 1970s **Doctor Who** was rising, perhaps partly in order to support this myth of creative decline.

---

[3] Quoted in Segal with Russell, *Regeneration*, p18.
[4] See for instance the skit 'The Pitch of Fear' from the BBC *Doctor Who Night* (1999).

Regardless of the fresh vision and creative impetus of seasons 25 and 26, the BBC capitalised on the wider public's perception that **Doctor Who** was no longer relevant. As an example, most of the casual audience and mainstream critics missed the cutting-edge political satire of *The Happiness Patrol* (1988), choosing instead to ridicule the Kandyman's appearance and his likeness to Bertie Bassett[5]. The BBC, buoyed by the fact that the cynicism extended to the fans, were happy to accept such a narrative as a useful explanation for the indefinite delay in commissioning a new series.

Despite the valiant efforts of John Nathan-Turner and Andrew Cartmel, **Doctor Who** never quite recovered from the perception that it could only appeal to dedicated fans. Back in 1982 when scheduling decisions had the power to make or break a series, BBC One controller Alan Hart had the foresight to move **Doctor Who** away from its traditional Saturday night slot following successful competition from **Buck Rogers in the 25th Century** (1979-81). Initially the move doubled the viewing figures, but with its general audience seemingly secured, Nathan-Turner made the fatal error of pandering to continuity-obsessed fans. Ratings dropped again,

---

[5] A view that was still being propagated in a 2002 episode of **Room 101**, in which Paul Merton conspired with Michael Grade to throw **Doctor Who** into the vault. The Kandyman is one of a number of creatures to be ridiculed in the process. It wasn't until 2010 that the story's political subtext reached the public eye. Cartmel (quoted in Adams, Stephen, '**Doctor Who** "Had Anti-Thatcher Agenda"') admitted:

> 'Critics, media pundits and politicians certainly didn't pick up on what we were doing. If we had generated controversy and become a cause célèbre we would have got a few more viewers but, sadly, nobody really noticed or cared.'

leading Hart to restore the show to its traditional Saturday night slot. Without the necessary support of a more family-friendly and inclusive approach, the resultant upturn was short-lived. Hart's successor Michael Grade, recognising that **Doctor Who** had lost its general appeal, altered the schedules again, putting the show up against **Coronation Street** (1960-) and into terminal decline. The long-overdue steps taken by the production team to broaden the reach of **Doctor Who** during the McCoy years (e.g. celebrity guest stars) were significantly hindered by the new transmission times. **Doctor Who** had effectively become a specialised subject, after the producer and the commissioners had in turn undermined each other's efforts to bring the show back into the mainstream.

As soon as it was announced that **Doctor Who** would be returning in a co-funded cross-Atlantic production, all the old myths about creaky sets and low-budget effects returned with a vengeance. Some critics were praising these as virtues, as if they were an essential part of the show's charm, others were hoping to see **Doctor Who** lose its 'here's one I made earlier' feel. Most agreed that **Doctor Who** had always been done on the cheap.

Jo Wright, the producer tasked with representing the BBC's interests in the venture, notes that an important part of her brief was to ensure that the production did not feel like the same show that had been cancelled in 1989: 'I'd been told very specifically not to connect what we were doing in any way with the series when it ended.'[6]

Of course, satirists aside, no writer or producer would ever want to

---

[6] Quoted in Handcock, Scott, 'Finding an Audience', *Doctor Who Magazine* (DWM) #497, cover date April 2016, p35.

make a show that was cheap, tired, irrelevant, self-congratulatory and fan obsessed, but what sets *The Movie* apart is that it was deliberately written to avoid those charges being levelled against it. Responses to each one of those complaints can be clearly seen in Jacobs' final script, even though the writer admits to having been unfamiliar with 80s **Doctor Who**[7].

Away with Wobbly Sets and Dodgy Effects

'...at worst, [**Doctor Who** was] the butt of a joke, usually one about wobbly walls or monsters proving unable to climb stairs.'[8]

[Jonathan Morris]

In reality the budget for *The Movie* still proved to be restrictive and when viewed against the convincing effects seen in season 26, with the exception of the TARDIS interiors the production values were hardly worlds apart. To maintain the illusion of a lavish production, Matthew Jacobs' story, prologue aside, is completely Earthbound and monster-free. Costume and stage design compensate for a lack of special effects, but the character-driven narrative has clearly been shaped by budgetary constraints[9]. The scale of the story is made to look grander than it is through the stock footage montage of New Year celebrations around the globe (with impossible synchronicity).

---

[7] See Appendix 2: Interview with Matthew Jacobs.
[8] Morris, Jonathan, 'I Came Back to Life Before Your Eyes. I Held Back Death...', DWM #497, p13.
[9] In his introduction to Jacobs, Matthew, *Doctor Who: The Script of the Film* (1996), Segal cites the budget as a secondary reason, behind the desire to tell a story that is personal to the Doctor (p vi).

The Revitalisation of a Spent Force

The pacing and tone of the episode are partly down to the seven-act Tuesday Night Movie format, but are also a throwback to the hijinks of the Pertwee era. As such, the script embodies the creative goal to supplant an albeit distorted impression of 80s **Who** with a return to the James Bond action-man version of the character[10]. The physicality of the eighth Doctor is heightened by the decision to portray his predecessor in the mould of a retired elder statesman, giving the impression, for those aware of the backstory, that his adventuring days with Ace are long gone, or even that he is redundant without his vivacious action woman by his side. The first adjective applied to the character in the script is 'weathered'[11], and in the press pack and onscreen credits McCoy is listed as 'the Old Doctor'[12]. The seventh Doctor is as tired as the BBC's view of the series itself. Out of adventures and almost completely passive, he has been reduced to a custodian, a taxi-driver and a puppet of the Master's. All this is the antithesis of where Cartmel was taking the character.

A Hero Fit for the Times

Relevance is established by the contrast drawn between Sylvester McCoy's and Paul McGann's Doctors. The former is not simply there to provide continuity for fans; he is used to represent the departure

---

[10] The sixth Doctor could be characterised as less active, with his verbosity and fondness for fishing, but the seventh Doctor, though often overshadowed by Ace's tendency to throw herself into the action, would frequently belie his diminutive appearance.

[11] Jacobs, *The Script of the Film*, p14.

[12] Similarly, Gordon Tipple is credited as 'the Old Master'.

of the old guard. This is a Doctor who in no way fits in, who is literally in the wrong place at the wrong time when he gets shot down. His TARDIS materialises in front of a poster of London with Chinese text above it – the familiar coexisting with the unfamiliar. When Chang Lee writes the Doctor's name on the hospital form, he doesn't settle for the standard American 'John Doe', but chooses 'John Smith' – perhaps because of the Doctor's accent, but still nonetheless a sign that Lee sees the stranger as completely alien to his world, a misfit from an irrelevant past.

By contrast, the eighth Doctor rejoices that his shoes fit. This is a Doctor who firmly belongs in this narrative world. He conforms to the notion of the romantic hero, charming yet mysterious, friend yet stranger, and intelligent yet naïve.

A Willingness to Break the Mould

Despite its fair share of 'Easter eggs', from jelly babies to the fourth Doctor's scarf, any sense that the show is unashamedly wallowing in its own past is completely undone when the newly regenerated Doctor shouts with primal rage 'Who am I?' It is the one question shared by fans and newcomers alive. For the former it marked a dramatic shift in how the Doctor is presented in the series, but one that has become a mainstay since the 2005 revival. In 20th-century **Doctor Who**, rarely are we given access into the Doctor's thought processes, and as a result his emotions are limited. Instead we share his companions' ignorance. There are notable exceptions (*The Green Death* (1973), *The Brain of Morbius* (1976), *Horror of Fang Rock* (1977), *Remembrance of the Daleks* (1988)) but by default the Doctor avoids questioning himself.

A post-regeneration crisis of one form or another had featured in a number of debut Doctor stories as a useful conceit for gently coaxing the viewer into accepting the new incumbent. Using such a series-based convention for a one-off feature would be highly problematic, however, since there is no room to bring about the required resolution for the audience. The eighth Doctor actually regains his memories efficiently and without relapse, but mention of his parentage and the emergence of certain unexplained new powers throws open the door to all kinds of retcons and revisionist interpretations of the character and the mythology surrounding him. The Doctor may have answered his own question, but we are none the wiser. Compared to the continuity-obsessed extremes of some of the late 1980s episodes the movie is a breath of fresh air, offering exactly the kind of vibrancy the BBC had been holding out for, but the novelty factor would have been completely lost on the uninitiated.

Reaching Out to the Mainstream

American fans will have been far more conscious of the switch to the mainstream than those in the UK. Having previously been aired on the Public Broadcasting Service (PBS) and targeted at a niche audience, the fact that **Doctor Who** was to be broadcast in a primetime slot on a major network made clear the lofty ambitions of the new production. In the UK, the BBC could rely on the curiosity factor to bring in a much larger audience than the show had been achieving at the tail end of its original run. Nevertheless, rather than schedule *The Movie* on a significant in-house date (such as the anniversary), the show was broadcast on a Bank Holiday and marketed as 'event TV'. With the Doctor gracing the cover of the *Radio Times* there could be little doubt that the BBC were marketing the movie for a mass audience[13].

The fact that those who had never seen the show before were expected to outnumber the fans had a significant impact on the script: 'Most people who see the film will have never seen **Doctor Who** before, so it's got to be accessible and understandable to a whole new audience.'[14] Philip Segal was clear from the outset that *The Movie* should not require a knowledge of **Doctor Who** mythology to be enjoyed.

A variety of techniques are employed to broaden the appeal of the story. With great economy the narrated prologue gives the lowdown on all the key aspects of **Doctor Who** mythology, even including the Daleks, who play no role in the story from that point on (other than being named by the Doctor, to Grace's bemusement). The odd piece of **Doctor Who** jargon is either avoided or translated (e.g. the TARDIS' chameleon circuit is described as a 'cloaking device'). Instead of drawing on past episodes of **Doctor Who** for tone and symbolism, more widely known myths and stories, both ancient and modern, are referenced, whether through dialogue, design, direction or musical cues: Frankenstein, Christ, the Terminator, Batman, **The X-Files**, **ER**, *Beauty and the Beast*, **Star Trek**, *Madam Butterfly* and Wild Bill Hickok to name but a few. All of this is more than simply a marketing

---

[13] The magazine made a similar front-page splash for 1993's Children in Need special, *Dimensions in Time*, but prior to those one-offs the Doctor had not featured on the cover since 1983's anniversary special *The Five Doctors* (itself a one-off, some 10 years after the end of the semi-regular appearances). The success of the show since 2005 is reflected in the number of *Radio Times* covers.

[14] Geoffrey Sax, quoted in *Radio Times*, 25 May 1996, souvenir pull-out p2.

strategy. It is born of an implicit criticism of the perceived irrelevance and self-referentiality of 1980s **Doctor Who** and a belief that the programme deserves a place in the mainstream.

Globalisation, Americanisation and a British Identity Crisis

We have seen how deeply *The Movie* was shaped by an almost pathological desire to avoid the negative perceptions that **Doctor Who** had received in the 1980s. But an equally pervasive influence was the impact of globalisation on British and American identity at the time. Segal describes his version of the show as 'international'. Jacobs talks about his memories of **Doctor Who** with nostalgic pride and likens the Doctor's sense of alienation in San Francisco to his own experiences of being a British immigrant in the States: 'I felt like I was half human because I was an alien in a foreign land, so I basically brought that feeling to **Doctor Who** that he is neither one thing nor another, neither alien nor human in a way.'[15] The clash of cultures is not simply a case of cause (the collaboration of the BBC, Universal and Fox), or effect (the ongoing debate about the Americanisation of **Doctor Who**); it is hardwired into the story as a major theme: 'The [eighth] Doctor serves as a repository of transnationalism, he is British, human and alien all in one.'[16]

The explicit references to the Doctor's Britishness are partly down to the author's personal experiences, but an underlying political

---

[15] See Appendix 2.
[16] Hellekson, Karen, 'Memory and the 1996 Remake of **Doctor Who**' in Lavigne, Carlen, and Heather Marcovitch, eds, *American Remakes of British Television: Transformations and Mistranslations*, p164.

dimension was also very much in play. At the time the UK government were treating its drama, comedy and entertainment exports as:

> 'part of a wider UK policy to embrace globalisation, free trade and international competitiveness in ways that placed the British creative industries on the world stage as a showcase for Britishness and British life.'[17]

It was no surprise that related policies proved to be short-lived. As early as the late 1960s British shows only tended to get picked up by the major US networks if signs of Britishness, such as references to contemporary British life, had been minimalised. Furthermore, in the 1990s, US networks, rather than buying British shows outright, were preferring to go down a co-production route in order to remain competitive in their own marketplace[18].

Any discussion of *The Movie* has to wrestle with the questions, 'Is **Doctor Who** an essentially British show?', and what it even means to be 'British' in such a context. Steven Moffat (executive producer 2010-17) maintains that the answer to the first question is yes, though he admits to not knowing what exactly that Britishness consists of:

> 'When you're exporting a show around the world, do you worry about how to appeal to other cultures? And I think the way to appeal to other cultures is to be your own culture, just to be yourself. And Americans **like** British shows. If they elect

---

[17] Steemers, Jeanette, 'British Television in the American Marketplace, in Lavine and Marcovitch, *American Remakes*, p9.
[18] Steemers, 'British Television in the American Marketplace, pp5-6.

to watch a British show, they want it to be terribly British… The Britishness of **Doctor Who** is sort of irrelevant to **Doctor Who** because it takes place in all of time and space. Whatever is fundamentally British about that mad show, it's just leaking onto the screen from the people that make it. It's not a calculated thing. I'd have to concede that there's something **incredibly** British about **Doctor Who**, but I couldn't necessarily say what it is.'[19]

When rumours of a Hollywood movie directed by David Yates surfaced, Steven Moffat was initially dismissive of the idea, arguing that it could only happen as a BBC-led project. His argument was one of continuity and brand ownership, but in clarifying his position he made this telling comment: 'I'm sure there's money to be made out of it but that's not the point, is it? We are British, the BBC. We are there for the art.'[20] Such a sentiment reflects the common fear that Americanisation leads to a dumbing-down of culture and art[21].

The exact same charge was being levelled against the BBC in the early 90s as by necessity it became a market-orientated global

---

[19] Quoted in Minkel, Elisabeth, 'The Global Force of **Doctor Who**.'
[20] Quoted in Leane, Rob, 'Doctor Who Film: Steven Moffat "Happy", But Must Not "Damage the Series"'.
[21] E.g. Janet Street-Porter (quoted in Lavigne, Carlen, and Heather Marcovitch, 'Introduction' to *American Remakes*, p ix):
> 'Britain and America have very different sensibilities. We are grown up, sophisticated, knowing and capable of layers of meaning… American culture is one-note. It tells you a story in a childlike, simple way and then clobbers you over the head with it time and time again.'

enterprise[22]. Huge discussions were taking place about how to preserve the Britishness of **Doctor Who** whilst honouring the non-British demands of the Fox network. Compromises were required on both sides, leading to an end product that was not entirely satisfactory to any party involved. In the end the Britishness of the Doctor was assumed to be a non-negotiable[23]. Superficial elements were included that associated the alienness of the Doctor with Britishness, such as his fondness for tea. At one point Grace even apologises for his actions by saying, 'He's British.'[24]

Critics argue that the eighth Doctor is an American stereotype, the kind that British writer-director Richard Curtis would play on to great commercial effect, and that most recently seen in the character of Newt in *Fantastic Beasts and Where to Find Them* (2016): 'McGann's Doctor represents an American idea of the modern British gentleman, courteous, well mannered and slightly foppish.'[25]

Further into this book we will consider what the British essence of **Doctor Who** might actually consist of, and how far *The Movie* continues in that tradition. Suffice to say at this point that it places such concerns at the heart of the adventure.

Millennial Fears

The turn of the millennium had long been the subject of apocalyptic fantasies amongst religious and cult groups, but during the mid to

---

[22] See Chapman, James, *Inside the TARDIS*, p174.

[23] On the casting of Paul McGann, Jacobs says that a decision was taken that the character (as distinct from the actor) would be British (see Appendix 2).

[24] All quotes are taken from *The Movie* unless stated otherwise.

[25] Chapman, *Inside the TARDIS*, p178.

late 1990s the world was gripped by the fear that civilisation, now heavily dependent on computers, would be thrown into chaos because programmers had failed to account for dates beyond 31 December 1999. Various worst-case scenarios were drawn up in the event of 1999 being followed by 1900. Chemical plants might explode, aircraft might crash into each other, life-support machines might switch off, nuclear missiles might self-launch and – seemingly of equal concern – interest rates might be miscalculated. With the threats of the Cold War and terrorism lessened, or at least left as the sole preserve of conspiracy theorists, the fear that the world could be destroyed by accident took their place in our imagination.

Throughout the 1990s environmental disasters and end-of-the-world scenarios were popular themes for Fox's Tuesday night movies[26], and in 1996 a number of big-screen apocalypse stories were at various stages of development[27]. In setting the story on 31 December 1999, with a scenario that on the stroke of midnight the world would end, Jacobs could not have made **Doctor Who** more current. This aspect of the story, whilst secondary to the epic conflict between the Master and the Doctor, will have been a key selling point, particularly as far as Fox were concerned.

---

[26] E.g. *Deadly Invasion: The Killer Bee Nightmare* (1995), *The Invaders* (1995), *Tornado* (1996).

[27] *Independence Day* was released that year and would be followed by *Armageddon* (1998), *Deep Impact* (1998) and *Dogma* (1999) among others.

HE'S BACK – BUT IT'S ABOUT HOW
A Remake or a Continuation?

Before reaching the scripting stage a number of decisions had to be made as to how *The Movie* would sit in relation to the previous series. Firstly, it needed to be established whether this version of **Doctor Who** would be a remake or a continuation. The feature-length format, the move to a transatlantic co-production and the fact that the mainstream audience would consist of a large number of people who had never seen the original, all suggested that a remake would be the most profitable approach. But the following factors pushed in favour of a continuation and ultimately outweighed those marketing and consumer considerations:

- **A Question of Timing.** Whilst **Doctor Who** fans may have felt that it was an age since the last **Doctor Who** episode had aired, the first moves towards its return were taken almost before the paint had dried on Nathan-Turner's last season. A gap of seven years is a relatively short one between a show's cancellation and relaunch[28]. The longer the break, the more likely a series will receive the full-on reboot treatment.

- **The Lack of an Origin Story.** Unlike many superhero narratives, and rebooted shows such as **The Bionic Woman** (2007, originally 1976-78) and **Battlestar Galactica** (2002-09, originally 1978-80), **Doctor Who** has

---

[28] Most relaunched shows began at least 10 years after the original, with the longest gaps being **Burke's Law** (1963-66, 1994-95) (28 years) and **Twin Peaks** (1990-91, 2017) (26 years).

never had an origin story at its core. The Doctor's past and the roots and motivations behind his powers, ethics and travels are shrouded in mystery throughout its original run. The American love for an origin story made **Doctor Who** an ideal candidate for a prequel rather than a reboot, because retelling **Doctor Who** from scratch would beg the question, 'Where do you start?'

- **Reinvention is an Essential Part of the Show's Logic**. With the snake-like ability to periodically shed its own skin and start afresh, **Doctor Who** has never maintained a consistent narrative. Change is built into the fabric of the show's mythology with the concept of regeneration. On the face of it, a remake ought to present less controversy for **Doctor Who** fans than would be the case for virtually any other series. An individual actor, for example, is not intrinsic to the series in the same way that Keifer Sutherland was to **24** (2001-10, 2014)[29]. But if the Doctor's ability to regenerate was considered a unique selling point, then all the origin elements that the new target audience might hanker for could be subsumed into a regeneration story. It meant that *The Movie* could offer a distinctive voice whilst also remaining part of the show's continuity.

- **Competing Visions and the Fear of Being Excluded**. If *The Movie* failed to generate a new series then as a remake it would have risked being disconnected from the whole and being ignored by any future revivals of the series. At

---

[29] A fact borne out by the poor reception of **24: Legacy** (2017).

best it would be treated as a curiosity in the same way as the Peter Cushing movies[30]. **Doctor Who**'s cult-like status would ensure that the series would live on, whether through future series, movies or other formats such as Virgin Publishing's **New Adventures** range of novels. To be part of that rich history, *The Movie* had to avoid being seen as a reboot in case it failed. If a new series had been greenlit from the outset we might well have seen a complete reset, with McGann being written as the first Doctor (Mark II). Posterity-wise, as a one-off a remake made little sense.

- **The Rights Issues. Doctor Who** is complicated somewhat by the fact that the BBC do not own all of the most iconic properties of the show. Any remake would be caught between having to use the Daleks conservatively to gain the approval of Terry Nation's estate, or ignoring them altogether and thus becoming an entirely different show. For the remake to be seen as such, it must include variations on the most essential elements of the original. **Doctor Who** without the Daleks and the Cybermen would be like **Battlestar Galactica** without the Cylons, or **24** without Jack Bauer. Furthermore, the BBC itself, whilst wanting to steer the franchise away from the 80s, was keen to preserve what it viewed as non-negotiables, such as the external appearance of the TARDIS as a police box. A continuation, no matter how revisionist, could maintain the Britishness of the brand and protect the BBC's

---

[30] *Dr Who and the Daleks* (1965) and *Daleks' Invasion Earth 2150 AD* (1966).

commercial interests more effectively than a complete reboot. The timing that year of the BBC's trademark application for the police box exterior of the TARDIS is no coincidence. If it was to eventually drop its partnership with Universal, then the corporation would need to ensure the show remained profitable in other ways.

A Very Good Place to Start?

Once it had been established that *The Movie* would be part of the same narrative universe as the original, Segal had to decide whether to pick up the series where it left off, with or without a gap in time, or write it as a sequel or a prequel. The idea that the show could spawn a sequel was first mooted by William Hartnell with his suggestion of a 'Son of Doctor Who' series[31]. He was of course envisaging his retirement, and assumed that when he quit the role the character of the Doctor would be finished with. A 1990s sequel to **Doctor Who** would have depended on the series having had a definitive ending, which might or might not have resulted in the death of the Doctor. McCoy's final voiceover in *Survival* (1989) has the opposite effect to, say, the dramatic conclusion to **Blake's 7** (1978-1981). It is at one and the same time a farewell speech and a tease that at some indefinite point the show would return with the Doctor as the lead protagonist:

> 'There are worlds out there where the sky is burning, where the sea is asleep and the rivers dream; people made of smoke and cities made of song. Somewhere there's danger,

---

[31] Letter to a young fan, reproduced in Haining, Peter, *The Nine Lives of Doctor Who* (1999), p35.

somewhere there's injustice, and somewhere else the tea is getting cold. Come on, Ace, we've got work to do.'[32]

Had the next **Doctor Who** story been the first of a new series on BBC One, we could imagine the writer symbolically referencing this quote with, for example, a burning sky in the opening shot, or a discarded cup of tea. We almost get both by sheer coincidence, only the sky in question is the flaming eyes of the Master, and the tea belongs to the Doctor, in keeping with the psychological and biographical nature of the piece. With the Doctor still on his travels offscreen, and not in a grave or back home on Gallifrey, a sequel would need to start with an ending, or at least make reference to one. It would inevitably confuse the new audience and alienate the core fans.

Starting from the very beginning was initially seen as the most logical approach, as evidenced in the two prospective scripts that preceded Matthew Jacobs' involvement. The story behind the Doctor's flight from Gallifrey was still waiting to be told, making it the ideal starting point for a new audience. It was only a minor inconvenience that mystery was built into the very fabric of the original show, as represented by its name. The name could be literalised if need be or turned into a question that could be answered. Fans could either see William Hartnell as a future incarnation of the Doctor, or reconcile the difference through the concept of alternate universes. When it comes to **Doctor Who**, an origin story is far from a de facto reboot.

Philip Segal's initial approach to the BBC in 1989 did not spell out his vision for the series in story terms. Instead the preliminary discussions revolved around the commercial and financial aspects.

---

[32] *Survival* episode 3.

When formally expressing his interest in developing **Doctor Who** for an American audience, the only content issue the producer raised was the nationality of the Doctor[33]. Segal was eager to gauge the BBC's attitude concerning the potential casting of an American actor in the role.

For his part Roger Laughton, then a director at the BBC, also sidestepped any talk of specific content, advising Segal that any deal (which at this stage would have been struck with Columbia) would depend on the corporation receiving assurances that 'a relaunched **Doctor Who** can have the maximum impact while retaining its **Doctor Who**-ness.'[34] It is a strikingly nebulous and ill-defined term, suggesting that the powers that be had little idea what the show's unique character consisted of, or indeed what it was they were trying to recapture and protect. Significantly, in an early stage of the negotiations the BBC turned to the show's first producer Verity Lambert to act as go-between[35], assumed to be a safe pair of hands as far as preserving the essence of **Doctor Who** was concerned.

Segal responded by reassuring Laughton that he intended to retain the 'spirit' of the show, again without specifying in any way what that 'spirit' consisted of, but at this point, in a veiled critique of 80s **Doctor Who**, he made it clear that he would want to prioritise and control story content[36]. Perhaps anticipating some resistance to this latter point and to illustrate that the kind of narrative threads he had in mind would not be of a completely novel quality, he requested a copy

---

[33] The letter is reproduced in Segal with Russell, *Regeneration*, p6.
[34] Segal with Russell, *Regeneration*, p12.
[35] Segal with Russell, *Regeneration*, p15.
[36] Segal with Russell, *Regeneration*, p13.

of *City of Death* (1979), praising it as exactly the kind of story that American audiences would lap up. In the end the BBC were unwilling to relinquish all creative input, pointing out that their preference was for a co-production deal and not a licensing arrangement.

The various twists in the tale over the next few years are well documented, but it is important to note that at no point does there seem to have been any substantial unpacking of terms such as '**Who**ness', 'spirit' and 'Britishness'. All three were effectively banded about as ciphers for 'consistency', yet there were no agreed definitions in place. The lack of frank and thorough discussions over content is all the more remarkable given the levels of anxiety at the BBC over the representation of the brand and by association, itself. Focus centred around hiring individuals who, as reliable keepers of the tradition, would keep a check on any unwanted excesses or deviations, from actors and advisors to the producer himself[37]. The closest we get to any real indication of the BBC's expectations over content can be seen rather obliquely in the steps they took to clarify the copyright holders for existing creatures and characters from the **Doctor Who** universe, including the Daleks, who were one of the few elements the BBC had insisted upon.

Drawing up a bible to sell a new series to prospective networks is standard practice, but in order to keep story at the heart of his enterprise, Segal hired screenwriter John Leekley to pen the words and production designer Richard Lewis to furnish it with lavish illustrations. The bible is not simply an introduction to **Doctor Who** to a new and unfamiliar American audience, it is the means by which

---

[37] The BBC even made it a condition going forward that Segal remained as producer (Segal with Russell, *Regeneration*, p20).

Segal could convey the essence of the show as he saw it.

Leekley's script was an extension of his work on the bible, a large section of which was devoted to the world building of Gallifrey. The origins of the Doctor had become the heart of the narrative, not so much in the form of a reboot but, in Leekley's own words, 'a pre-conceiving' of the established mythology[38]. After Leekley was moved on from the venture, a second attempt was made to sell a script based on the series bible. Replacement writer Robert DeLaurentis was instructed to stick with the origin element to the story[39].

Moving away from the mythological tone and epic scope of the original, DeLaurentis' story was potentially more accessible to new viewers. By grounding his narrative in relationships and personalities he was able to add a lighter, personal human touch. Characters were less one-dimensional, with DeLaurentis going into far more detail in the planning process about the Doctor and the Master's qualities, introducing layers of ambiguity and rough edges to the heavily typological figures that Leekley had envisaged[40]. And yet the script was deemed to be even less effective than Leekley's. Certainly Segal was deeply critical, fearing that it had completely lost connection with what the show was about: 'we ended up so far away from the heart and soul of **Doctor Who** that it was painful.'[41] The observation is damning, especially given that DeLaurentis' brief was to rework the

---

[38] Lofficier, Jean-Marc, *The Nth Doctor*, p226.

[39] Lofficier, *The Nth Doctor*, p260.

[40] He suggested that the Master needed to be more intelligent and surprising and the Doctor should be more human and infused with a 'Holmesian' quality (*Doctor Who: The Complete History* #47, pp53-54).

[41] Segal with Russell, *Regeneration*, p37.

Leekley script precisely in such a way as to recapture the lost charm of the original series. Even with the backing of Jean-Marc Lofficier in his capacity as 'fan liaison' and continuity adviser, once the somewhat shoehorned and forced continuity aspects were removed from the equation[42], this particular origin tale amounted to a complete reimagining[43].

Segal's revival of **Doctor Who** finally found a new home on Fox's Tuesday night movie schedule, with Fox executive Trevor Walton giving the green light to Segal even before a script had been approved. Whereas the Leekley script had been written in tandem with the bible as part of the pitch for the networks and as a pilot for a new series, the replacement could be written without the added pressure of selling the entire concept of **Doctor Who**. The writer would instead be presented with the challenge of scripting a story that could work as both a one-off and a 'backdoor' pilot, though the creative impact of the latter tends to be overstated. In effect, the finished product would be the sales pitch and so the script had to be written as a single drama rather than a lead-in to a new series.

By deciding to accept Walton's offer, Segal effectively sacrificed his plans for a new series. Some **Doctor Who** was better than no **Doctor Who**, even if *The Movie* might only spawn other movies rather than the preferred option of a full series. Exaggerated talk of the backdoor pilot was useful only insofar as it might be a softener to the BBC, who

---

[42] Ironically at Lofficier's suggestion (*The Complete History* #47, p58).
[43] After the idea of introducing a completely different type of Dalek, one created by and subservient to the Master, was abandoned, rather than substitute them for another classic villain (Lofficier suggested the Ogrons) Delaurentis reconceived them as a new race of cyborgs, the Zenons (*The Complete History* #47, p59).

had envisaged **Doctor Who** as a continuing drama[44]. Unsurprisingly then, by resigning himself to this risky strategy instead of persevering with network serial departments, Segal could no longer treat the Leekley bible as a 'live' document. There was simply too much backstory and world-building to fit into a one-off movie format. Unlike DeLaurentis, Jacobs was offered the chance to start more or less from scratch, with a set of briefing notes replacing the bible and existing script treatment.

Had *The Movie* been primarily treated as a pilot episode, then the origin story would not have been ditched in its entirety. Time would have been spent to introduce worlds and characters at the expense of pace, focus and direction. Over the course of an entire series continuity could emerge. It would start with a very clear fresh departure but bit by bit, episode by episode, begin to weave the new elements into the old[45]. Caught between continuation and introduction, between appealing to passionate fans and reaching out to an entirely new audience (now brought into even sharper focus by its broadcast not only on a major network but in a primetime TV slot), it could only be written as the next chapter in the ongoing adventures of **Doctor Who** – a self-contained story in keeping with

---

[44] Segal's fear of the BBC's response to any moving of the goalposts was palpable – note his delay in informing them that Spielberg was no longer connected to the project. On the DVD documentary 'The Seven Year Hitch', Segal explains that the notion of the backdoor pilot came about because he called in a favour from a friend in the Fox serials department. There is no indication that this was ever a serious prospect.

[45] Which is effectively the approach taken by both Russell T Davies and Steven Moffat.

the episodic nature of the original series, and one lacking an ongoing arc or any unresolved plotlines to be carried over. Of course, the competing demands of appealing to fans and newcomers would have been present in any pilot, but there was a real danger now that in marketing **Doctor Who** as a movie the eighth Doctor would be regarded as a quirky one-off like Cushing. Segal risked being seen as a tribute act and not the latest in a long line of producers. Establishing *The Movie*'s potential to be part of a continuing drama required retrofitting it into the previous season since it could hardly foreshadow a future that was far from guaranteed. Ironically, those links to **Doctor Who**'s immediate past were among the most difficult elements to sell to the BBC.

Setting a New Perspective on the History of Doctor Who

Having opted for a continuation of the original series rather than a reboot, and having decided to write it as the next chapter in the story as opposed to a sequel or prequel, Segal then needed to establish how *The Movie* would channel the parent show. It was a three-way choice between parody, deference and perspective shift. Would the movie be based on the skewed 1990s impressions of **Doctor Who**; camp, low-budget and quasi-British? Certainly this would set a distinctive tone in contrast to the overly serious nature of much of American sci-fi at the time, for which 'Humour need not apply, [because] these are stories of life and death, dark and unpredictable.'[46] Science fiction series had moved in two opposing

---

[46] Garcia, Frank, and Mark Philips, *Science Fiction Television Series, 1990–2004: Histories, Casts and Credits*, p7.

directions: niche and complex fan-pleasing fare such as **Babylon 5** (1993-98); and multi-genre series like **The X-Files** (1993-2002, 2016-18), aimed at bringing sci-fi firmly into the mainstream by combining its traditional themes and patterns with elements of police procedural drama, medical dramas and soap opera. The odd quirky episode aside, the chief exemplars of both approaches reflected a shift towards more complex characters, more ambiguous villains, and more believable scenarios.

The BBC would certainly not have entertained the notion of parodying their own property, particularly as several key voices in the corporation felt that to its detriment **Doctor Who** had been doing exactly that during the 80s[47]. From an American perspective, however, the quirkiness of **Doctor Who** was part of its unique appeal, including its tendency to not take itself too seriously. Both the Leekley and DeLaurentis scripts fell short on exactly that front. It was vital that the show had a distinctive tone, simply because of the sheer number of competitors in the market at the time. Between 1959 and 1989 some 62 new science fiction shows aired on US networks. Between 1990 and 2014 that number had nearly doubled[48]. Only around 50% of these shows were granted a second series[49]. In such a climate it is little wonder that Segal, Jacobs and director Geoffrey Sax all saw mileage in emphasising the lighter, more comedic aspects of **Doctor Who**.

As far as the Fox network was concerned, the Britishness of the show

---

[47] They would only begin to do so after the expiration of Universal's option on a new series.
[48] Garcia and Philips, *Science Fiction Television Series*, p10.
[49] Garcia and Philips, *Science Fiction Television Series*, p6.

and its longevity were both unique selling points, but a more thoroughly parodic approach would surely have brought even greater attention and recognition. Many critics of *The Movie* found themselves nostalgically yearning for the series' old fashioned, wobbly set charm[50]. Furthermore, the distinctly British humour of Rob Grant and Doug Naylor had already turned **Red Dwarf** (1988-1999, 2012, 2016-17) into a surprise hit stateside. Their British 'underdog' mentality paradoxically brought international success and mainstream recognition. By contrast there was an ambitiousness behind the concept of *The Movie* that bordered on the pretentious, based on the implicit assumption that **Doctor Who** could trade on its past successes and that all it really needed was an injection of cash and a bigger audience.

Humour is nonetheless a key part of *The Movie*'s tone, and indeed would have been more so had the BBC not pulled so tightly on the reins. Geoffrey Sax, perhaps somewhat defiantly, describes the final piece as a comedy thriller[51]. The humour here is far from satirical, contributing to the overall innocent tone, even when the jokes are adult. We are never laughing at the characters, not even the Master when he is at his most flamboyant. When Jacobs does throw in a reference to the show's past it is always respectful and never comes across as a send-up. He avoids, for instance, a dig at the more outlandish costumes of past Doctors, even as the eighth Doctor discards the scarf. The humour is largely confined to witty exchanges,

---

[50] E.g. Mike Hughes is one of many critics who at the time equated big budget with Americanisation: 'If you like spectacle, you'll love this. If you like **Doctor Who**... well, move to England, which has more wit and less whoosh' ('"Blue" Cop Sags Tonight').
[51] Gillatt, Gary, 'Renaissance', DWM #238, p12.

mostly deliberate on the speaker's part, though Jacobs also makes great mileage out of the Master's ignorance of Chang's street language.

While there is little evidence of the parodic in *The Movie*, it can hardly be described as being deferential to the show's history. Jacobs resisted becoming overly weighed down by matters of continuity, and was happy to introduce a number of new additions to the myth such as the relocation of the Eye of Harmony from Gallifrey to the Doctor's TARDIS (c.f. *The Deadly Assassin* (1976)), the TARDIS' sentience and healing powers, the Doctor as half-human, the Doctor's regeneration being preceded by death, and the Doctor being theoretically able to alter his species through regeneration.

Jacobs avoided too much digging into the show's back-catalogue (he hardly had the time) and relied instead on his childhood memories. Shaped by those accumulated experiences of watching **Doctor Who** Jacobs 'wrote what [he] wanted to see'[52]. Philip Segal provided the initial guidelines as a replacement to the extensive (in his own words, 'overblown') bible, setting out the key premise and the main themes and characteristics he was looking for[53]. Segal reimagined the movie as a journey of self-discovery. The quest to find the Doctor's father had been internalised into a quest to recover his memories and sense of self following the amnesiac effects of his regeneration. The briefing notes provide a much greater level of insight into the

---

[52] Gillatt, Gary, 'Urban Regeneration', DWM #239, p12. He did however consult Lofficier's *Doctor Who: The Universal Databank* (1990) as an aide-memoire or fact checker when necessary (*The Complete History* #47, p62).

[53] The notes are reproduced in Segal with Russell, *Regeneration*, pp98ff.

thinking behind *The Movie* than the Leekley bible, of which only the bare minimum had been carried forward.

In terms of the history of **Doctor Who**, Segal's briefing notes single out William Hartnell as a blueprint for the new Doctor, but there is no mention of the Master or the name 'Gallifrey'. The home of the Time Lords and the Doctor's background are no longer to be conveyed on screen, but are to be referenced in the process of the Doctor remembering who he is. Segal stresses that the story needs to be a simple tale of personal awakening, placing the focus on the Doctor's character and nature and away from much of the mythology of the show. The original Gallifreyan use of the name 'Doctor' in its more generic academic sense, a point made specific in the Leekley script, is eschewed in favour of the medical connotations of the word. The eighth Doctor is essentially one who heals (see McGann's final line in his only other onscreen appearance in the role, in 'The Night of the Doctor' (2013)). Segal determined that the story should revolve around the Doctor finding his healing powers all over again as he sets about trying to save present day Earth from an alien threat. In place of the Master, Segal discusses the Daleks in some length, not because he wants Jacobs to include them in the script, but to give some clues about how to write a contemporary equivalent – a new enemy to bring the show into the 21st century, one that will hopefully become as iconic as its Skarosian forebears.

The Doctor as set out in the briefing notes is a hero invested with certain powers by virtue of being a Time Lord, but he is not a superhero who lacks weaknesses, flaws or gaps in his knowledge and understanding. He must have the capacity to grow and develop. From all the notes Jacobs had received, this observation became the starting point for his script. Turning on its head the cause-and-effect relationship between the Doctor fixing something and remembering who he is, he summed up his thinking in the tagline: 'Only when Doctor Who knows who he is will he be able to save us all. Only if you know yourself can you save yourself.'[54] This observation provided the basic structure behind the movie, one that preceded the more detailed breakdown into seven acts. The movie is essentially in two halves – the Doctor rediscovering who he is and the Doctor saving the Earth. Although slightly more contrived than the idea that the Doctor remembers in the act of becoming a saviour figure, the advantage of such an approach is that Jacobs could more easily mirror the audience's own journey from ignorance to knowledge of the Doctor. The Doctor's growing realisation of who he is can effectively become the psychological equivalent of an origin story.

Segal wanted Jacobs to make the Doctor's humour the most appealing aspect of his character, the kind of hero who is underestimated and dismissed as a buffoon. Unlike Superman, who completely sheds his Clark Kent persona when on the job, the Doctor's humanity is not a disarming disguise but an essential aspect of who he is. His charming, almost childlike naivety is partly born out of an alien ignorance of our ways and customs, but it is also the result of his flawed idealism and optimism. Much of the humour of the script revolves around Grace's exasperated reactions to her alien friend's strange and unsettling ways.

Doctor Who Am I?

This focus on the nature of the Doctor is what gives *The Movie* its unique perspective on **Doctor Who**. Ambiguities around the Doctor's

---

[54] Jacobs, quoted in Segal with Russell, *Regeneration*, p100.

character had been built into the show from the beginning. While the Doctor had been originally conceived of as an alien, the 1960s scripts never clearly established the fact, allowing for the possibility that he was a human being, albeit an 'out of time' one from a distant colony. His ability to regenerate is the first thing that sets him apart physiologically, but writers mostly avoided explicit references to his alien nature and background until it was time once again to replace the lead actor[55]. In *Spearhead from Space* (1970) he had two hearts and was very clearly not of this world, forced to live among mortals in punishment for his benevolent interventionism.

Whilst the Doctor's alienness is expressed through his love-hate relationship with planet Earth, particularly in the Jon Pertwee era, until *The Movie* the Doctor's disconnectedness and experience of being 'other' was a subject that the writers steered clear of. The closest we get to the Doctor questioning who he is comes from those post-regeneration stories in which he needs time to adjust to his new body, namely *Castrovalva* (1982) and *The Twin Dilemma* (1984). Although the character is introduced in 1963 as unreliable and bows out in 1989 under the unsettling shadows of his alien morality and ulterior motives, such avoidance of existential anxiety is consistent with the unquestioning attitude towards the Doctor's heroic status that dominated the middle years of the original series like an overfilled sandwich. To express doubts or uncertainty about who he is runs hand in hand with a lack of assurance over his morality. The Doctor cannot be seen to question himself without the viewer being

---

[55] Notable exceptions include *The Evil of the Daleks* (1967) where he is revealed to lack the 'human factor' and *The Tomb of the Cybermen* (1967) where he mentions his extraordinary age.

led to do the same.

In *Castrovalva* the Doctor is immediately aware of who he is meant to be, but uncertain that the process will be successful: 'I'm the Doctor. Or will be, if this regeneration works out.'[56] In order to take ownership of his new body he must disassociate himself from his former self. To symbolise the need to break free from the ghost of his fourth incarnation the Doctor unravels the iconic scarf, albeit to repeat a pragmatic trick from the legend of Theseus and the Minotaur. When the thread has all gone he continues to shed his predecessor's costume, removing his shoes and then cutting up the less iconic waistcoat (though its association with the fourth Doctor is highlighted by a reference to one he left on Alzarius, the planet on which the fourth Doctor met Adric in *Full Circle* (1980)). With Tom Baker establishing himself as the definitive incarnation of the Doctor due to the popular appeal of his early years and his longevity (he would have been the only incarnation many viewers had seen), it was arguably more important than ever to set the new Doctor free from the shadows of his predecessor. To that end, the confused fifth Doctor begins to channel each one of his past lives, highlighting the fact that Tom Baker was one among many. After his recuperation in the zero cabinet is cut short, whilst admitting to not really knowing who he is, the fifth Doctor at least remembers that he has come to Castrovalva in search of a Doctor (a quite intentional irony).

At the end of the story we the viewers are invited to join Tegan, Nyssa and Adric in accepting the Doctor's new face and continuing on our travels with the enigmatic Time Lord. Reassuringly he feels like his old self, but immediately qualifies that statement 'Well, whoever I

---

[56] *Castrovalva* episode 1.

feel like, it's absolutely splendid. Let's go.'[57] *The Movie*, in prioritising new viewers over those familiar with the series, does not need to be so insistent on the fact that the eighth Doctor is different from but nonetheless still the same man as his predecessor. With the assumption that the majority of the viewers will have few or no preconceptions about who the Doctor is, the Doctor's post-regeneration amnesia is written as if he is discovering who he is for the very first time. His recovered memories are not related to his previous lives as seen in the BBC series, but to a distant past that predates his departure from Gallifrey and to various offscreen encounters[58]. References to Jo Grant, K9 and Romana would have been lost on viewers unfamiliar with the series, but Freud, Marie Curie, Da Vinci, and Puccini are all well-known figures, even if by name only.

The Twin Dilemma follows the pattern of *Castrovalva* by presenting the Doctor as undergoing an existential post-regeneration crisis but nonetheless still knowing that he is the Doctor. With Peri struggling to understand, having been totally unaware of the Doctor's ability to regenerate, the Doctor assures her 'I'm not people, Peri. I happen to be me.' Again, the emphasis is on distancing him from his predecessor, this time through the conceit of his being overly harsh in his self-assessment:

---

[57] *Castrovalva* episode 4.
[58] A point inadvertently strengthened by the production team's failure to gain clearance to use images of all seven of the Doctor's previous incarnations in the scene in which the Master tracks the eighth Doctor down using the Eye of Harmony (Geoffrey Sax's comment in Segal with Russell, *Regeneration*, p119).

DOCTOR

My last incarnation, I was never happy with that one.

PERI

Why ever not?

DOCTOR

It had a sort of feckless charm which simply wasn't me.[59]

The Doctor's sickness gives him an overinflated ego and more frivolously, by his own admission, a terrible dress sense. At first the viewer is led to believe that despite his statements to the contrary he is far from being himself, a fact highlighted by his inability to understand Peri's compassion and forgiveness. Significantly however, at the conclusion of the adventure, with the Doctor confirming that the side effects of regeneration are over, his continued rudeness is directly associated with his alien nature: 'You seem to forget, Peri, I'm not only from another culture but another planet. I am, in your terms, an alien. I am therefore bound to different values and customs.'

The questioning of the Doctor's character post-regeneration is an inconvenient side effect for the Doctor, who fears he is 'falling to pieces', but for Peri and the viewers it is a reminder that regardless of the state of his health he is not one of us. We are left with no choice but to put up or switch off: 'Whatever else happens, I am the Doctor whether you like it or not.'[60]

---

[59] *The Twin Dilemma* episode 1.
[60] *The Twin Dilemma* episode 2.

The Doctor's jubilant affirmation of who he is in *The Movie* is a personal victory, a moment of realisation that restores his zest and affirms both his alienness and his familiarity. It is therefore quite different from his 'I am the Doctor' assertion in *The Twin Dilemma*, which is entirely for Peri and the viewers' benefit.

By effectively reimagining the Doctor's ability to regenerate as a rebirth, fully aware that in so doing he was departing from canon (as confirmed by the Doctor's theory that he was 'dead too long this time'), Jacobs is able to fuse the idea with the traditional elements of an origin story. Paradoxically the Doctor becomes both Frankenstein and Frankenstein's monster in the process. The Doctor's questioning of himself up until this point in the show's history had always been based on specific actions (*Genesis of the Daleks* (1975), *Horror of Fang Rock*). Even when regeneration threatens to destroy him psychologically, the Doctor is never deeply existential or ponderous. He knows who he needs to be and who he wants to be. He also knows, in however muddled a way, who he used to be. Following Segal's recommendation that references to Gallifrey should be part of the Doctor's journey of self-discovery, Jacobs writes the eighth Doctor as if he is starting from a clean slate, beginning with the restoration of his earliest memories.

The above observation raises the question of why Jacobs was so keen to give Sylvester McCoy a prominent role in the drama (though one confined to the first, albeit longest, of seven acts)[61]. Segal had

---

[61] A common misconception is that the seventh Doctor is around for far too long, but his onscreen time is disproportionately short compared to his importance to the plot, creating a somewhat false perception.

imagined the story beginning with the Doctor already on Earth, having travelled here knowing that he is about to regenerate. He would have selected the Earth as the best place to convalesce during the expected post-regeneration sickness[62]. Already it is clear that whilst the Doctor might be starting from scratch, the show certainly is not. Introducing not one, but two new Doctors would have potentially undermined the novelty and marketability of Paul McGann as **the** next Doctor and so Jacobs' choices were limited. The only viable alternatives were to either begin the drama with the regeneration itself in mid-process (concealing McCoy's face from the start) or with the Doctor having already undergone the transformation, (explaining Time Lord physiognomy in the form of a voice-over prologue). Fudging one of **Doctor Who**'s most distinctive and unique features was hardly an appealing option with the audience expecting spectacle[63]. Furthermore, a regeneration scene would be perfect as the lead in to the all-important cliff-hanger into the first ad break ('Who am I?').

McCoy then, had to feature, but he does so in the most pedestrian of ways, unsurprisingly given that he had effectively been cast to help sell the products on display in the first interval and to highlight how tired the 1963-89 series had become in the eyes of its commissioners. On this reading the casting had little to do with a desire to please the fans, even though Jacobs is eager to point out that he made the decision as a fan. The fact that a McCoy appearance

---

[62] In both *Castrovalva* and *The Twin Dilemma* the Doctor has specifically travelled to a place where he can be healed.

[63] It works in *Rose* (2005) because the effects of the Doctor's recent regeneration are hardly profound (other than an observation about his ears, the Doctor is untroubled by his new appearance).

appealed to so many fans was an added bonus which producer Philip Segal was quick to capitalise on as part of his active courting of the fans[64].

McCoy's role, whilst physically prominent, is lessened both by the fact that Jo Wright would only entertain the notion if he had few or no lines, and by Jacobs making him a victim with limited agency from the outset. In his first script outline, contrary to Segal's briefing notes, it is the Master who has set the TARDIS to land on Earth, and in later drafts the TARDIS itself. The trigger to the Doctor's regeneration is no longer the result of old age, with the attendant degree of control it allows him over the precise moment of his departure. In Jacob's original outline the regeneration is loosely described as having been caused by the Master's direct intervention, and is subsequently written as the ironic consequence of Grace's attempt to save his life. The seventh Doctor, the master manipulator, has been reduced to a victim of circumstances beyond his control, a fact made doubly apparent by the reason for his hospitalisation in the first place.

The popular argument that it would have been prudent to have introduced Paul McGann from the outset (as with Christopher Eccleston in *Rose* (2005)) is based on a number of flawed assumptions. Firstly, as we have seen the intention was not to pander to fans. Secondly, the original extended and unaired version of the shooting lacks the feeling that it had been rushed (if anything it is too protracted, hence the cuts)[65]. Thirdly, whilst the seventh Doctor's

---

[64] Even to the point of claiming credit for the decision: 'I simply had the script written that way' (Segal with Russell, *Regeneration*, p135).
[65] Another reason being a particularly unconvincing scream by McCoy. For a detailed breakdown of the cuts and accompanying

specific role in the theme of the Doctor learning who he is, is indeed largely superfluous, he is intimately connected to the story in other ways; most notably the character of Chang Lee, who would have required a complete rewrite if the character were removed, since he plays an unwitting part in the Doctor's fall. The idea that the seventh Doctor's appearance was a mistake is also not borne out in the findings of a survey of audience views of *The Movie* carried out for this book[66]. The two most memorable scenes both involved McCoy (the shooting, the regeneration) and the character was generally well received by established and new fans alike. In fact, despite his being barely recognisable from the seventh Doctor of the Virgin **New Adventures** line, those who were fully invested in those ongoing stories gave the most positive assessment of McCoy's role in the movie[67]. A certain air of gravitas is unintentionally conveyed by the Doctor's silence, allowing the messy nature of his send-off to be overlooked.

---

screen shots, see 'The 1996 TV Movie' on The Millennium Effect website.

[66] See Appendix 1.

[67] See Appendix 2.

COMING TO AMERICA: REDEFINING THE BRITISHNESS OF DOCTOR WHO

'If you want to sell a show to the world, make it as British as you can. America likes **Doctor Who** because it's British. Do what it says on the tin. It would be insane to make **Doctor Who** less British.'

[Steven Moffat][68]

Steven Moffat, while overseeing a period in which **Doctor Who**'s global reach had been wider than ever, nonetheless routinely promoted the essential Britishness of the show as its biggest selling point. The effect of Americanisation on British culture and **Doctor Who** in particular continues to be a subject of much highly-charged debate, long after Segal's ambitious attempt to resurrect **Doctor Who** to America had fallen by the wayside.

As the most extreme example of the two cultures combining in **Doctor Who**, *The Movie* sheds much light on how Britishness is defined and mediated through the programme, as well as the effects of globalisation and Americanisation on the character of the show. Yet despite the movie's explicit privileging of Britishness, Danny Nicol's 2018 dissertation on Britishness in **Doctor Who** as a whole lacks any notable references to the production or story[69]. One possible explanation for this odd omission is that Nicol excludes from his study any elements of British culture that he considers to be non-political, such as the emotional restraint conveyed by the term 'stiff

---

[68] Quoted in Harrison, Andrew, 'Steven Moffat: "I Was the Original Angry **Doctor Who** Fan".'
[69] Nicol, Danny, *Doctor Who: A British Alien?* (2018).

British upper lip'[70]. *The Movie* prioritises the personal over the social. Structural or societal evils such as repressive governments or greedy multinational corporations, so often the focus of the Doctor's ire, are entirely absent from the story. However, by Nicol's own admission, 'Britishness' as a term is intrinsically political and the lack of political and social engagement in the script of *The Movie* is in itself a political act. Besides which, as we shall argue, the Britishness of the Doctor in the movie runs far deeper than his English accent and fondness for tea.

Doctor Who's position as an icon of Britishness is reinforced by frequent comparisons to the American **Star Trek** franchise, thus the insider/outsider debate is often framed in terms of British versus US science fiction, rather than say British versus European, or West versus East. But just how sharp is the distinction between what is British and what is American? There is an unfortunate propensity for critics to create soundbites in which largely artificial and contrived divisions do little more than reflect discriminatory ideologies. In 2007, for instance, Caitlan Moran patriotically declared:

> 'That a children's sci-fi show, made on what amounts to a minuscule budget, **in Wales**, by gays, should be one of the defining programmes of the 21st century, is just the kind of thing that makes Britain great. You'd never get the Americans knocking out a show about a 900-year-old pacifist with a magic screwdriver, whose biggest enemy is a set of giant, fatal pepperpots.'[71]

---

[70] Nicol, *A British Alien*, p31.
[71] Moran, Caitlin, 'Torrid in the TARDIS'.

The unease with which many in Britain greeted the news that **Doctor Who** would be remade for an American audience reflected long-held anxieties about the loss of national identity. As far back as 1924 DH Lawrence suggested 'all this Americanising and Mechanising has been for the purpose of overthrowing the past.'[72] In the 1920s, despite the proliferation of American products and fashions in Britain, the movie industry bore the brunt of anti-American sentiment. Some of the criticism was down to sheer elitism, but there was a degree of justification to the fears, given that the Hollywood movie industry was explicitly used as a tool to sell American culture, ideals and products to the world[73]. Perceived differences between British and American sci-fi reflect the contrast between British concerns over its Empire-building history and America's assertive self-promotion, as well as their respective projections. To put it crudely, the British sci-fi hero explores and observes whilst the American conquers and interferes[74].

In reality **Doctor Who** started life as a hybrid show, born out of the coming together of British and North American creatives and sensibilities. As such '**Doctor Who** had found its niche as a British character living American B-movie adventures.'[75] The Doctor, whilst reflecting values, tastes and concerns that could be defined as

---

[72] Quoted in Campbell, Nick, Jude Davies and George McKay, eds, *Issues in Americanisation and Culture*, p13.

[73] See Glancy, Mark, *Hollywood and the Americanisation of Britain*, p21.

[74] See Plauche, Geoffrey, 'American vs British Science Fiction.'

[75] Cull, Nicholas, 'TARDIS at the OK Corral', in Cook, John R, and Peter Wright, eds, *British Science Fiction Television: A Hitchhiker's Guide*, p55.

British, has always been, at least in intent, a transnational explorer with no fixed abode – 'a citizen of the universe, and a gentleman to boot.'[76] The debate about whether to observe or intervene is a fundamental aspect of the series, with the Doctor flitting between both sensibilities. Nonetheless his allegiances are heavily biased towards the human and in a narrower sense, particularly (though not exclusively) in relation to earthbound adventures, he and his companions are cast as the representatives of Britain on the international stage. Even here however, there is room for debate, with the show consistently prioritising southern England to the extent that the term 'British' is often mistakenly used interchangeably with 'English'[77].

There are plenty of examples of this false equation in the making of *The Movie*. In the tie-in novelisation, Gary Russell, working from an earlier version of the script than the one released by BBC books, has Grace apologise to the police officer because the Doctor is 'English'[78]. If former residents of England should have known better, then how much more so Alan Yentob, who in the notorious unscripted telephone call at the end of the documentary *30 Years in the TARDIS* (1993) expressed his wish for the Doctor to be played by an

---

[76] 'The Feast of Steven' (*The Daleks' Master Plan* episode 7, 1965).

[77] As Nicol observes, while the revived series reflects a more positive presentation of the other nations of the UK, particularly post-devolution, the classic series was more prone to English biased stereotypes. Even so, there remains a firm bias to the South of England, with the first Northern companion, Clara Oswald, relocated to London (Nicol, *A British Alien*, pp83-112).

[78] Russell, Gary, *Doctor Who: The Novel of the Film*, p134. When they were still involved in negotiations, Columbia even described **Doctor Who** as 'the London series' (Segal with Russell, Regeneration, p14).

Englishman?

This skewed definition of Britishness does a disservice to the original series, for whilst there is some merit to the view that prior to 2005 the Doctor had historically been characterised as the 'English gentleman,' appearances and accent aside, as soon as that phrase is unpacked we are in territory that could be extended to a British sensibility as a whole. Indeed, to speak of Englishness as a nationality is itself problematic[79].

The Movie styles the Doctor around the English-born tradition of the Byronic hero. Fashion and presentation aside, such a character is an iconoclast, a thorn in the side of the status quo and a reminder that Britain is a nation of hybrid peoples who value non-conformity and resist homogenisation. The English bias that presents the Liverpudlian McGann as hailing from the south of England, slightly hamstrings Segal and Jacobs' avowed intention to return the Doctor to his rebellious roots, with their version of the Byronic hero virtually indistinguishable from other romantic types in his embracing of Britishness as Englishness. If anything the eighth Doctor more readily reflects the 'feckless charm' of the most English and least Byronic of Doctors, the cricket-loving fifth. Ironically, it is the proudly Scottish 12th Doctor who is the most Byronic of them all.

Steven Moffat's belief that Americans are passionate about British television is born out by the sheer number of British shows that have

---

[79] English nationals have always been less likely to identify themselves as English instead of British than are the Scottish or Welsh. See the comparative survey findings in Heath, Anthony, and Jane Roberts, 'British Identity: Its Sources and Possible Implications for Civic Attitudes and Behaviour', p6.

been broadcast or remade for an American audience over the years. As John Patterson puts it, 'If there were such a thing as an equivalent to the Chinese stranglehold on the American economy, the hands around America's cultural throat would be British.'[80] However, British themes and qualities, whilst appealing to niche audiences, were hardly conducive to the mainstream. With American television less likely to want to ape or idolise British shows in the 90s, **Doctor Who**, despite the best intentions of the BBC, would find it impossible to buck the trend to assimilate. Back in the UK, the political pressures placed upon the BBC to present their products as beacons of Britishness to the world stood in polar opposition to the aspirations of the American networks and production companies.

This fraught situation presented several issues to Matthew Jacobs. On a practical level it meant that following the late rejection of the Leekley and DeLaurentis scripts, he had an incredibly short window to come up with a fully-scripted workable alternative. Despite the lack of time, Jacobs' work was still subject to intense scrutiny from the various interested parties, with the BBC taking a particularly deep interest in the script. The situation was only properly resolved after the writer travelled to England to iron matters out face to face. The script was still being tinkered with well into the filming. Though this was by no means a unique situation, given the sheer number of competing interests the whole project was in danger of becoming completely fractured and incoherent. The fact that Jacobs was still happy with 60 to 70% of the final version should be viewed as a success, at least as far as those involved in the project were

---

[80] Quoted in Lavigne and Marcovitch, 'Introduction' to *American Remakes of British Television*, p xi.

concerned[81].

Traces of the incomplete nature of the final script are not hard to detect. To be fair most of the flaws are based on non-ideological, practical hurdles. Presumably with more time, following the decision to replace the expensive *Turandot* aria with 'Un Bel Di' from *Madam Butterfly*[82], the discussion of the Doctor having been present when Puccini wrote Turandot would have been replaced with a reference to the latter. The opening narration, hastily rerecorded with a voice over from Paul McGann instead of Gordon Tipple, would have been more effectively scripted so as to tie in better with the resolution of the plot. When Eric Roberts found his prosthetics too uncomfortable, there was insufficient time to revise the script to include non-visual reminders that the Master's borrowed body was degenerating. As a result the sense of urgency behind his quest to steal the Doctor's lives is somewhat lacking. Above all there is a rushed and confused air to the ending, brought about largely because Jacobs had understandably not pictured the cloister room as a huge cathedral-like space. The unscripted choreography of the final battle needed to be carefully stage-managed in order to utilise as much of the expensive set as possible.

None of the above difficulties can be directly attributed to any ongoing debates about the essence of **Doctor Who** and in particular its Britishness. Whilst such ideological questions ought to have been discussed in great depth, throughout the process they remained hidden behind the specifics. There was an unspoken assumption that the Americans would protect their interests and the British theirs. At

---

[81] A point he makes in 'The Seven Year Hitch'.
[82] See Appendix 2.

the very least the politics of power and control created a degree of tinkering for the sake of tinkering over plot and characters, as if simply by having more input over the script the BBC could indeed make it more British. Ironically, it could be argued that Segal's vision was more British than theirs, perhaps down to the BBC all-too-easily acquiescing to the mistaken belief that big budgets and special effects improved a show by default. This scrutinising of the script as a story by several BBC representatives meant that that less care was taken in ensuring that other potential shortcomings were either prevented or fixed.

British Objections to the Jacobs Script

A closer inspection of each of those elements in Jacobs' draft scripts that the BBC objected to suggests that despite the lure of America and the potential for the BBC to achieve global recognition, the political drive to retain the Britishness of the show was very much at work, whether surreptitiously or sub-consciously.

The Doctor Is Too Attached to Earth

In keeping with Segal's brief, Jacobs avoided the heavy reliance on mythology so redolent in the Leekley script by making the Earth central to the story. The BBC were of the opinion that this move had led to an insufficient focus on the Doctor's alien qualities. Whilst not completely discounting the idea that that the Doctor might have a human mother, Jo Wright suggested that the focus on his human side be toned down[83]. Jacobs had not only proposed to make the Doctor half-human, he had specifically written British DNA into the Doctor by scripting his mother as a British woman from the Edwardian era.

---

[83] Segal with Russell, *Regeneration*, p108.

Whilst such an idea could be seen as a metaphor for the show's British origins, in writing his mother as a figure from the past there was a danger of the Britishness of **Doctor Who** being seen as old-fashioned, based on a heritage view of Britain's distinctive qualities – a far cry from the cosmopolitan and post-colonial reality. The move would have inadvertently symbolised the idea that Britain was the past and America the future for the show, reflecting the BBC's greatest fears about the co-production deal. Thus it was in the interests of the British to write out the Doctor's British mother.

In the 1990s, Britain was fully signed up to the values of neoliberalism, and nostalgia for the mythical closed borders of the past had yet to bite. Throughout the classic series, the Doctor had for the most part reflected that spirit of internationalism, with narrow-minded British politicians and civil servants the objects of ridicule[84]. It is notable that the post-9/11 disillusionment with Britain's courting of the international stage brought to the 21st-century series a far greater degree of patriotism than in the original run[85]. But back in 1996, the BBC, in seeking to ensure that the alienness of the Doctor is emphasised in *The Movie*, were promoting British values of tolerance, openness and internationalism. At the same time it was important not to define the Doctor in terms of American patriotic sensibilities, even if in the Doctor's case they would have been expressed as British rather than American. Britain may have been on

---

[84] Nicol highlights the 1970s trust in internationalism over narrower British sensibilities as evidenced in UNIT and the Doctor's repeated struggles against British bureaucrats (Nicol, *A British Alien*, pp128ff).
[85] Nicol argues that the revived series is Eurosceptic by omission (p50), hostile to Americanisation and multinational corporations, and far more brazenly British than the original series had ever been.

the verge of 'Cool Britannia', but it was not quite ready to proudly fly the union jack.

Do We Really Need a Car Chase?

It might at first seem somewhat odd that of all the elements in the script the BBC should be terribly concerned about a car chase. When asked about what input the BBC had had on the script, Matthew Jacobs first recollection was of protracted debates over a sequence that had been written to show off the spectacular terrain of San Francisco and its surroundings. He goes on to concede that the criticism that the production had overly Americanised **Doctor Who** was a valid one[86]. But could a car chase really be seen as more American than British? After all, it would certainly not have been the first time it had happened in the show (see in particular *Planet of the Spiders* (1974)). Was the BBC nervous about overselling San Francisco in the story? There may be some truth to this, given that a compromise was reached whereby the shortened chase took place on more generic and flat streets (much to Jacobs' disappointment). That said, the BBC had no issue with the prominent use of the iconic Golden Gate Bridge.

The concerns over the car chase need to be seen as part of the BBC's wider observation that too much of the plot revolved around the Master and the Doctor playing a game of cat and mouse. The BBC also wanted the Doctor's journey of self-discovery to be slowed down[87], so by cutting some of the frantic and more superfluous action scenes additional space could be left to focus on the Doctor's

---

[86] See Appendix 2.
[87] Segal with Russell, *Regeneration*, p108.

awakening. This fitted in well with Jacobs' vision of the point of the story and suggests that the chase scenes were initially more about the writer fulfilling the expectations of the American audience, a concern that the BBC had largely disregarded.

It's All Too Camp and Arch

We have already noted the comedic elements to *The Movie*, but without the BBC's intervention this aspect of the drama would have been even more pronounced. The use of the word 'camp' to express their concerns reflects the BBC's narrative that **Doctor Who** had partly lost its way by becoming just that[88]. Whilst the show had been quite prepared to satirise itself (see especially the literal cliffhanger to episode 1 of *Dragonfire* (1987)) the BBC were not interested in sending up what they hoped would be their most profitable export. Any hints of a lack of reverence to the central concept were to be removed at all costs, and so too any reminders of how the British public perceived **Doctor Who** in the late 80s. Camp was being used here as a byword for a cluster of disparaging assessments, from corny and pantomimic, to self-ridiculing and insincere.

After the failure of this attempt to bring **Doctor Who** back to its glory days as essential family viewing, all these criticisms so prevalent during the dying embers of the original show were reeled into the thoroughly satirical *The Curse of Fatal Death* (1999). It was as if by commissioning the parody, albeit for Comic Relief, the BBC had given up on any aspirations to resurrect the series. Until that point parody

---

[88] E.g. The BBC objected to the morphant snake crawling into the Master's mouth on the grounds that it verged on the 'camp' (Segal with Russell, *Regeneration*, p108).

was completely off limits[89].

For Matthew Jacobs however, bringing **Doctor Who** to an audience completely unfamiliar with the show even in its heyday demanded that he made analogies and references to properties well known in popular American culture, from the dark and brooding to the irreverent – nothing was off limits. One such property was *Bill and Ted's Excellent Adventure* (1989). The cult teen movie spawned a sequel, a Marvel comic, an animated series, a live action show (also broadcast by Fox), video games and even a short-lived cereal product. Almost universally panned by critics for its bawdy and frivolous humour it nonetheless captured the imagination of cinemagoers and launched the career of Keanu Reeves. As a rare example of American satire, albeit in its most unsophisticated form, the characters even became hosts of an annual Halloween special in which the top-selling movies of the year would be the subjects of parody.

Had Matthew Jacobs originally named the two morgue attendants Tom and Jerry, or Fred and Barney, instead of Bill and Ted it is unlikely the BBC would have been quite so critical of the 'schoolboy' humour. The direct association between the two shows (already linked through Bill and Ted's time machine, a 1980s US phone booth[90]),

---

[89] A documentary to open a season of repeats on BBC2, *Resistance Is Useless* (1992), made the fans rather than the show the object of parody in the form of the 'anorak' **Doctor Who** obsessive. The short film, despite including clips of some of the more infamous examples of campness, is respectful to its source material.

[90] The producers have always claimed the association was unintended, and that their original idea was kyboshed because of similarities to the DeLorean in *Back to the Future* (1985). However,

whilst a harmless in-joke, would have no doubt irked the BBC representatives given their sensitivities towards parodic treatments of the series. Other examples of the BBC suspecting that Jacobs was sending up the series include their strong dislike for a joke about Time Lords having two dicks[91]. Whilst some adult humour is retained (e.g. the double entendre about the size of the chip), the comedic elements at times feel tacked on rather than integral to the style.

Concerns Over the Characterisation of the Master

The BBC found the characterisation of the Master to be the most unsatisfactory element of the show, so much so that Jo Wright even suggested that Segal hire an additional writer to provide a more coherent villain[92]. The morphant snake form was considered to be confusing and Wright was concerned about a lack of motivation and explanation for his actions. In particular the reason for his rivalry with the Doctor was not spelt out. The moral and ideological differences between the two Time Lords were lost in the detail. One of the distinctive features of **Doctor Who** had been its memorable villains, who more often than not were ciphers for social ills and fears among the British population. The Master, while second only to the Daleks in prominence, was too complex and ambiguous a character to be generalised into a personification of evil per se, and it is clear that the BBC found it hard to imagine a **Doctor Who** adventure that lacked any ideologically driven corporate or state-induced villainy.

---

it's hard not to see the direct reference to **Doctor Who** in the scene in which a crowd try to squeeze inside the tiny booth.
[91] The joke would wait for Jackie Tyler to make it in *The Christmas Invasion* (2005).
[92] Segal with Russell, *Regeneration*, p110.

Such tropes had far greater potential as metaphors for Britishness than did the personal rivalry between two Time Lords. An in-depth focus on the characters' respective states of mind would have been more appealing had it been accompanied by more explicit clues as to how their divergent worldviews and attitudes had been shaped in the first place[93]. The half-human aspect was in theory a perfect explanation, but it came across as little more than a half-theory, with the post-regeneration vision of the Doctor's mother lacking the necessary foreshadowing and follow-up to be effective and affecting. The double movement of the Doctor's alienness in relation to Earth and his humanity in contrast to the Master's monstrousness had the unfortunate effect of each cancelling the other out.

Question Marks over the Mixing of Genres

The representatives of the BBC expressed some hostility to the extended hospital scenes, wryly observing that it came across like an episode of **ER** (1994-2009). The fact that they specifically referenced the US show rather than their own **Casualty** (1986-) would suggest that this concern fell into the wider fear of Americanisation. This paranoia was second only to the fear that the movie might reinforce the show's poor image and reputation by association with the McCoy years. In reality, as we have pointed out above, the fusion of genres was an essential element of sci-fi's entry into the US mainstream. It was also an effective way of keeping down the costs. The setting and

---

[93] The novelisation includes one such extra clue in an additional exchange (inserted by Gary Russell) in which the Doctor explains to Grace that he and the Master were once like brothers, united in their frustrations with the Time Lords and quest to find answers away from Gallifrey (Russell, *The Novel of the Film*, p153).

accompanying tone ought to have been viewed as an important device in broadening the appeal of **Doctor Who** to its wider target audience; instead it was frowned upon simply because it did not 'feel' like what **Doctor Who** was all about. Perhaps more importantly, it took away from the Britishness of the show. Setting the adventure in San Francisco was one thing, but too much focus on the everyday workings of an institution reflecting the American healthcare system was quite another. It is worth noting that the National Health Service has been long associated with Britishness[94]. From a British point of view it was less alien to relocate an NHS hospital to the moon (in the distinctly British-titled *Smith and Jones* (2007)) than to have the Doctor treated in an American hospital.

The desire to present the show as distinctly British conflicted with the desire to set the movie apart from the 1963-89 series. There was an assumption that increased production values were all that was needed to expel the ghosts of the recent past. Too much creativity at a story level was generally regarded with unease. In effect, the co-production was considered beneficial to the brand only insofar as it could provide a budget that could place **Doctor Who** on a par with its American competitors. Disappointingly, in the wake of the failure of the movie to generate a new series, the BBC made explicit its belief that for the series to ever return it would require a huge budget. The sentiment did not sit easily with Philip Segal. It was almost as if *The Movie* had not happened when just two years later David Thompson announced his plans to develop a BBC Films movie that would be a 'lavish reincarnation... without the wobbly cardboard

---

[94] A fact highlighted by the centrality of the NHS to Danny Boyle's London Olympics opening show (Nicol, *A British Alien*, p6).

sets of old. There is obviously a great movie to be made from **Doctor Who**.'[95] Clearly in the minds of some, despite its cinematic feel and the efforts to pull **Doctor Who** back into the mainstream, *The Movie* had failed to establish clear water between itself and the perceived failings of the original series.

What is so British about Doctor Who?

In 2011 the Arts Council-funded Icons Project published a list of 100 icons of England as nominated and voted on by members of the public. The result is an eclectic mix in which 'queuing' is sandwiched between 'stamps bearing the Queens head' and 'roast beef and Yorkshire pudding', '*Sergeant Pepper*', the 'seaside pier' and 'Sherlock Holmes'[96]. Only two TV dramas made the cut – **Coronation Street** and **Doctor Who**. The soap opera makes perfect sense, both in terms of the characters and settings it presents and the way its stories are told, but **Doctor Who**, a show about an alien traveller in time and space that can be completely different in tone from one adventure to the next? The obvious link between the two programmes is their longevity (with the exception of Monty Python, all the other fictional works and characters in the top 100 have a long history – Winnie-the-Pooh, Sherlock Holmes, *Lord of the Rings*, James Bond, *Pride and Prejudice*, Beatrix Potter and the works of Charles Dickens), but even so, to beat the likes of Shakespeare and CS Lewis to the cut is quite a feat. **Doctor Who**'s appearance on a list about English icons partly reflects the English biases of the original series, but though many of the icons are exclusively English, a

---

[95] Quoted in Norton, Charles, *Now on the Big Screen*, p253.
[96] 'Icons of England: The 100 Icons as Voted by the Public'.

number would, like **Doctor Who**, be better described as British.

Throughout its history **Doctor Who** is presented as British by association, with the Doctor an exemplar of how the British people should act within their own borders, and how they can influence those outside for the better. In *The Movie* the Doctor agrees with Grace's off the cuff 'He's British' in a stereotypically British way, conceding 'Yes, I suppose I am,' with a mixture of pride and reserve. This line would have made more immediate sense had the scenes with the Doctor's British mother not been cut, but as it stands we are forced to ask: in what way does the Doctor perceive himself as British? Is it, at the most simplistic level, because he is the star of a British-born TV show, a statement of roots rather than identity? To unpack this further we would need to look both at those qualities that are said to typify the British and at how Britishness has been defined in film and TV, with a particular focus on the 1990s. British identity is neither fixed nor monolithic; there is something quite nebulous and transient about it as if crisis and provisionality are built into its very personality. There are however a number of consistent threads that might help us to evaluate the extent to which **Doctor Who** in general and *The Movie* in particular reflect a British sensibility.

Hybridity

Through the years the Doctor has been at one and the same time a fictional, symbolic continuation of the old mentality of the Empire, and an agent provocateur, dismantling orthodoxies and exposing the questionable ethics of the colonialist quest and its successor, neoliberalism. He can be a destabilising, rebellious voice from the margins and the wilderness, but also a moralising lawgiver from the elite and the metropolis. Duality is in itself an essentially British characteristic – one that finds its expression in a curious and frustrating mix of the irreverent and the respectful, the self-effacing and the arrogant, the mysterious and the straightforward, and the liberal and the conservative. If there is an overarching Britishness in the Doctor it is his eccentric unpredictability, a trait that can easily be mistaken for hypocrisy.

In the original run of the series the reasons for the Doctor being impossible to tie down are never made explicit; at best they are brushed aside as being a consequence of his alienness. The revived series internalises that feeling of not quite belonging, so that it forms part of the Doctor's psyche and not simply a description of how he is (or wants to be) perceived by humans. In series 8 he is pushed into an almost Jekyll and Hyde level of duality. *The Movie* offers an optimistic alternative in which the Doctor asks that most fundamental existential question 'who am I?' and finds the answer in the realisation that he is half human. Earlier versions of the story would have made this a powerful turning point in the Doctor's story, with the vision of his mother triggering his buried memories. The original idea as conceived by Segal and Leekley was even more dramatic, with the Doctor finding out for the first time that his mother is human.

To be sure, even as the script stands there should be no ambiguity over the matter: both the Doctor and the Master confirm it and to retcon the Doctor's throwaway line as a joke ignores the centrality of his hybrid self as a key driver of the plot. That said, of all the scenes to have been written out of the script, the Doctor's vision of his mother was central to the structure and meaning of the story. By effectively removing a key supporting wall, the viewers were left to either piece the plot back together again or accept this controversial addition to the myth alongside an unsatisfying and incomplete story. In narrative terms, if the Doctor is not half-human much of the plot is nonsensical. After the Master makes the discovery and exclaims 'No wonder,' no explanation is given to Chang Lee as to what he means and yet those two words tell the viewers that it must be significant. What exactly does it make sense of for the Master – is it the Doctor's fondness for the human race, something the Master has certainly mocked him for in the past[97], or is it a distinctly human aspect of the Doctor's character the Master has in mind, or his unorthodox ways, or his identity issues when it comes to embracing his Time Lord status?

Perhaps the answer is meant to be found within the boundaries of the story: is this the reason why the TARDIS has selected the Earth for an emergency landing, or is it bound up in the Eye of Harmony and the fact that it requires a human eye to be opened? Since the movie makes no mention of Rassilon other than on the TARDIS destination display, are we meant to conclude that the Doctor's parents were its creators? This would at least make sense of the Doctor having unsuccessfully attempted to open the Eye in the past – perhaps it was something he had seen his mother do. It would also explain why the Master puts that failure down to the Doctor being 'only half' human.

Whatever the answers, the significance of the revelation has to be inferred by the viewers. Largely due to its novelty, the majority of

---

[97] The line is replaced in the novelisation with 'Of course. That explains so much. His obsession with this dreary planet especially.' (Russell, *The Novel of the Film*, p109).

fans have treated the idea as flippantly as the Doctor appears to[98]. By switching the revelatory aspect from the Doctor to the Master, the potential is there for further revelations when the rivals finally meet up. It is unbelievable that the Master would not at least have broached the subject. At a push this oversight could be attributed to the desperate nature of the Master's plight, but if he has time to play dress up, he clearly has time to grill or tease the Doctor about his dual identity. Instead, all he says is that he doesn't like the planet, without any effort to make this a personal attack on the Doctor. Furthermore given his allergic reaction to the human body he is inhabiting, was it of no concern to him that the Doctor's body is half-human too?

The seventh Doctor insists repeatedly that he is 'not human', and even after apparently confirming that he is half-human, the eighth Doctor continues to talk about the planet as if it is not a part of him. Grace too sees him as completely alien when she observes 'I finally met the right guy and he's from another planet.' Once the Earth has been saved, the Doctor shows Grace Gallifrey, calling it 'home' and when Grace admits that she will miss him, the Doctor jokes, 'How can you miss me? I'm the guy with two hearts, remember.' He leaves Grace and the viewers reason to think that he is going to his real home, but asks the TARDIS 'Right, where to next?' rejecting both Earth and Gallifrey as final destinations.

Clearly then, the script subverts its own logic by simultaneously revealing and concealing the Doctor's humanity and his dual nature. Whilst the BBC did not rule out the Doctor's hybridity, it was largely

---

[98] The majority of our survey respondents discount the possibility that the Doctor really is half-human – see Appendix 1.

their input into the scripting process that led to its reduced impact[99].
As a Brit living in America, Matthew Jacobs identified with the duality
of the Doctor and that sense of belonging yet not belonging that,
whilst more extreme for those living offshore, is a fundamental part
of British identity. Ironically then, on this front an important aspect
of the Britishness of the show is undermined by its British
stakeholders in their quest to promote Britain globally.

Brain over Brawn

Britain is often presented idealistically in **Doctor Who** as the
champion of the underdog, a 'tiny, damp little Island' (*The Empty
Child* (2005)) that through sheer bloody-mindedness and a refusal to
give up triumphs against the odds. Conveniently forgetting its
imperialistic past, Britain functions as a symbol of non-violent
resistance from the bottom up. Romantic notions are prevalent: the
real heroes of war as those who were simply surviving on the streets;
the defiant martyrdom mentality in the face of stark 'conform or die'
scenarios; the manipulation of the aggressors into destroying
themselves, etc. Such ideals are often accompanied by a debunking
of military solutions.

That spirit of non-violence is sometimes depicted satirically as
buffoonery and being out of one's depth, particularly as far as the

---

[99] For instance, when discussing with Trevor Walton the romance
between Grace and the Doctor, Jo Wright commented, 'just my luck...
the first time I've met the kind of intelligent man I've been looking
for, and he turns out to be an alien' (*The Complete History* #47, p84).
In correspondence for this book, Matthew Jacobs recalls Walton
passing this line onto him. In the final script the punchline is
(somewhat tellingly) changed to '...from another planet'.

elite are concerned, and when governments are involved in acts of aggression they are often presented as being under the influence of an alien power. Particularly in the revived series, the Doctor positions himself against any 'might is right' philosophies. His sonic screwdriver, once nothing more than a scientific instrument that did what it said on the box, becomes a symbol of his pacifism, his weapon of choice that can perform all manner of tricks to avoid violent confrontation.

The recent 'Who Against Guns' campaign drives home the politics of **Doctor Who**'s Britishness. The show is used to challenge the insufficient safeguards and inadequate regulations when it comes to the availability of guns in the US. *The Movie* throws the unarmed Doctor into a gun battle, and later has him turn a gun on himself to the bemusement of a police officer, immediately after agreeing with Grace that he is British. Real world events gave added poignancy to the Doctor's actions as far the British audience were concerned[100], and though it meant cutting down even further the gun battle scene, it heightened the impression that the Doctor's Britishness is expressed as an aversion to guns and violence.

The Doctor has often attempted to reason with the enemy in an effort to get them to stand down, and true to form he tries to make the Master see the contradictions between his methods and his goals: 'You want dominion over the living, yet all you do is kill.' The observation highlights the futility of war and the illusion of control that characterises dictators. But the Doctor fails to offer him an alternative way of cheating death (despite the fact that he is standing

---

[100] The Dunblane massacre took place just two months before the show aired.

inside it) and there is no hint of the friendship that once existed between them. The Doctor stands for justice, and the Master cannot escape the punishment for his crimes. In this respect the Doctor can hardly been seen as rebelling against the ethics of divine retribution and the eye-for-an-eye violence of capital punishment[101].

The lack of satire in *The Movie* leaves us with a Doctor who is at his most conservative, a throwback to the days of the Empire when British values and culture were being spread as if they were morally superior to those of the colonised: 'We can perceive the Doctor as exporting Britishness throughout the cosmos, without the need for conquest and colonisation.'[102] The fears of globalisation and the rise of multinational corporations in the 1980s had begun to undermine **Doctor Who**'s internationalist leanings, but the re-emergence of long-buried fears of Americanisation was only just beginning to surface. In *The Movie*, the Doctor is an ambassador for Western values, asserting a role for Britain in the neoliberalist expansion, and reflecting in particular its special relationship to the US. The partnership between the BBC, Universal and Fox meant that **Doctor Who** was moving in the direction of the politics it had previously satirised.

Cool Britannia

1996 was a year in which Britain was experiencing a resurgence of national pride. A nation that was once embarrassed at displaying the union jack, bottling it up for the yearly Last Night of the Proms knees-up, had started to reassert itself in the face of perceived

---

[101] As Nicol argues, the Doctor often displays a dislike of the unlike, and is far from a pacifist (Nicol, *A British Alien*, p160).
[102] Nicol, *A British Alien*, p47.

Americanisation of the arts. Kick-started by the burgeoning Britpop phenomena, this mood of unashamed patriotism was seized upon opportunistically by both the government and the opposition. The Euro 96 football championships held in England a month after the screening of *The Movie* particularly inspired a wave of pride and confidence as far as the host country England and Scotland, a qualifying team, were concerned, leading to a greater identification with Britain and its individual nations. The movement, despite its leftish anti-establishment roots, was largely a Londoncentric affair as the political elite cosied up to grassroots creatives and made it part of their manifestos to appear to speak for the people. The then opposition leader Tony Blair is often credited as the architect of 'Cool Britannia', but it was actually John Major's government, specifically the Department of National Heritage, that first adopted the phrase for political gain[103]. The Prime Minister who had been pilloried for his skewed view of Britishness was now claiming to be the driving force of a cosmopolitan, optimistic creative boom – a vibrant, loud and colourful return to the 'Swinging 60s' that was actually worlds apart from his grey **Spitting Image** (1984-96) puppet.

The Movie was first aired in this climate, and though it predated the Labour government's drive to use the arts to promote Britain across the world as cool, it was written at a time when Britain had emerged from its post-Empire shadows to be seen across the world, particularly as far as arts and fashion were concerned, as youthful and trendsetting. It was actually the US ice-cream makers Ben and Jerry who first drew attention to the phrase with their new 'Cool

---

[103] See 'Cool Britannia: Where Did it All Go Wrong?'

Britannia' flavour[104].

The predominant image of the British man of the mid-1990s was laddish, brash and macho, with the contrived pseudo-feminist backlash, the 'ladette' not helping to subvert the idolisation of the 'men behaving badly' mentality. The assertiveness of this male stereotype finds its way into the characterisation of the eighth Doctor, wrongly viewed by one critic as evidence for Americanisation:

> 'Forget the fact he's from the other side of the galaxy, The Doctor is about as British as they come. Over the past 50 years he's been an integral part of the ever-changing (or should that be regenerating?) face of British men, mediating our style, attitude, and place in society... [In 1996] the Doctor is resurrected for the US audience. Unsurprisingly, he's recreated in the image of the hyper-masculine American hero. Don't be fooled by the English accent – he's strong-jawed, gets the girl, and is prone to motorcycle chases. Speaks volumes about what the Americans think of British men.'[105]

There was certainly nothing in this quote that a *Loaded* reader would have objected to at the time. The Doctor's sexuality, whilst not as big a departure from the 1963-89 series as is sometimes made out, is nonetheless one of the key ways in which the character's humanity is highlighted. In being made explicit (despite McGann's attempts to turn the passionate kiss in the script into something less intense and sexually charged), the Doctor's non-celibacy is confirmed. Time

---

[104] The phrase 'Cool Britannia' originated as the title of an obscure one-minute-long song by the Bonzo Dog Doo-Dah Band in 1967.
[105] Fordy, Tom, 'What Does **Doctor Who** Say About British Men?'

Lords, we learn, even share the same dick jokes as humans. Peter Wright reads the Doctor's relationship with Grace as a mark of his unabashed heterosexuality, making it a key peg in his general argument that because of the need to gain commercial appeal, *The Movie* had sacrificed the Doctor's British liberalism for an American conservatism[106]. The Doctor's heterosexuality is however an argument from silence, and in the context of 1996's less repressed Britain the character is certainly not acting unduly forward[107]. In fact, if anything Jacobs' Doctor is not macho enough to neatly fit the distinctly British 'one of the lads' role model. When, much to the ire of Philip Segal, McGann turned up on set sporting his newly cropped hair, he immediately decided to fit him with a wig to move him away from this more aggressive, less effeminate and unromantic look. The eighth Doctor could even be seen as resisting the laddish trend in his soft-spoken diffidence and his love for the arts. His enthusiasm for art for art's sake proved to be ahead of its time when the Cool Britannia tag was quietly dropped by Tony Blair in the wake of the failure of the Millennium Dome and growing criticisms of insincere opportunism and a dumbing down of the arts[108].

---

[106] Wright, Peter, 'Expatriate, Expatriate: *Doctor Who: The Movie* and Commercial Negotiation of a Multiple Text' in Hochscherf, Tobias, and James Leggott, eds, *British Science Fiction Film and Television: Critical Essays.*

[107] Aside from the Doctor's attraction to Grace, he also suggests that Eric Robert's camp Master reflects a pro-heterosexual stance where queerness is associated with evil perversions. Even dismissing the somewhat forced phallic reading of Bruce's possession, Wright's interpretation of campness also fails to stand up to scrutiny in its oversimplified equating of camp with gay.

[108] See Sillito, David, 'Rock 'n' Roll PM: Blair's Cultural Legacy.'

The British Eccentric

Bill Bryson's bestselling travel book *Notes from a Small Island* was published in 1995 and was hugely influential in the presentation of Britishness at the time. It offers a view of culture in Britain based on the author's farewell sojourn around the island before his return to his US homeland. A blend of anecdotes and observational humour masks the political nature of the enterprise as Bryson effectively writes to sell his version of the country, warts and all. The British people were especially taken by his satirical yet affectionate approach, and in a BBC World Book Day poll voted it as the book that best represents the nation. Bryson manages to find beauty even in the warts, and his prose is replete with superlatives about the British people, often at the expense of his US homeland, calling Brits 'the happiest people on the Earth.' No wonder the British took him into their hearts. With Bryson discovering that the British are quite content to laugh about the annoyances and idiosyncrasies of British life, latterly he has adopted a more critical, Victor Meldrew persona. But the Bill Bryson of 1995 is unreservedly positive, capitalising on the rising tide of patriotism in the 1990s.

Whilst on his valedictory tour Bryson does highlight cultural differences between regions, his overall view of the British in 1995 is bound by a number of generalisations that bear little resemblance to the cosmopolitan and multicultural nature of most of its key cities. This is a Britain that captures the American imagination as much as it strokes the ego of the British. Eccentricity, puritanism, deference and taking pleasure in the inexpensive, small things in life, all form part of the predominantly English gentleman stereotype – the tea-drinking, biscuit-dipping Brit that America wants to believe in.

The Movie certainly panders to this stereotype. The eighth Doctor takes extraordinary delight in the fact that his new shoes fit, he doesn't seem at all driven by power or wealth, he wears make-do second hand clothes, he sees tea as a cure for ills, and he loves eating British candy from a paper bag. The jelly baby is more than simply a favourite form of confectionery for the Doctor, even if as far as the series goes it only came into its own after being used by Terrance Dicks to establish an obscure but fan pleasing connection between the newly regenerated fourth Doctor and the second Doctor. Thereafter it would often crop up as a symbol of the fourth Doctor's childlikeness (see for instance his grumpiness that there were no orange ones left in *The Invasion of Time* (1978)), but also of his distinctly British eccentricity and cunning, associated with various British traits such as brain over brawn (*The Face of Evil* (1977)), politeness (*The Robots of Death* (1977)), the mocking of authority figures and would-be-despots (*Destiny of the Daleks* (1979)), and black humour (*The Ark in Space* (1975)). It can be no coincidence then that in the novelisation based on an earlier script of the movie, the eighth Doctor tells Gareth that the jelly baby is an 'English delicacy.' [109]

This eccentricity is one of the few specific characteristics that producer Philip Segal described as British:

> '[**Doctor Who**'s] Britishness is what makes it work. The eccentricity of it is what makes it work. You can take that and plug it into any world, but you have to protect it and you have to leave it alone. Those American elements and the romance and all of the things that I was being forced to do... I think in

---

[109] Russell, *The Novel of the Film*, p162.

some ways actually hurt the character.'[110]

When it comes to unpacking just what is meant by the eccentricity of the British in relation to, say, the USA, it is usually described in list form as a series of quirky traits such as queuing, apologising, and discussing the weather[111]. For the British, the term is often used to refer to certain members of the aristocracy[112], but more generally speaking it is an adjective properly applied to anyone who stands out from the crowd on account of their whimsical character. Crucially, an eccentric can never be putting on a performance, otherwise they are dismissed as an attention seeker (in *The Movie*, the Doctor's natural eccentricity is in marked contrast to the Master's artificial, fraudulent showmanship). There has to be a naturalness to the eccentric's idiosyncrasies to be seen as someone born to be different. It is this latter form of eccentric that the Doctor had most often represented from 1963 to 1989, with arguably only the fifth Doctor channelling the more catch-all, watered-down term with his cricketer's outfit. In that respect it is unsurprising that the Davison Doctor is also the most diffident and polite of the bunch.

The eighth Doctor is characterised as eccentric mostly on account of his Britishness (the tea-drinking and the vast collection of clocks as a symbol for being old fashioned and quaint), resulting in a less outlandish figure than, for instance, the fourth Doctor, who is

---

[110] Quoted in Martin, Daniel, 'Who Do We Think We Are? **Doctor Who**'s Britain'.

[111] See for instance, the supposedly handy guide for foreign students '14 British Cultural Quirks and Eccentricities that May Take Visitors by Surprise.'

[112] For examples see Sykes, Tom, 'The Best Eccentrics Are British, Obviously.'

eccentric even by British standards. As a result, as far as the British are concerned, efforts to make the eighth Doctor stand out as odd are less than successful. The apolitical nature of the story also plays a role in softening this aspect of the Doctor's character. The eccentric explorer is one who finds truth and liberty by refusing to conform, a mindset which the eighth Doctor neither requires nor shows any sign of desiring. Peter Wright goes as far as arguing that after the Doctor has effectively restored the previous world order at the end of the movie, he is a 'spent force for social justice and reformation.'[113] Kevin Dekker suggests that the move away from rationalism towards romance and fairytale has blunted the teeth of **Doctor Who**'s social commentary: 'Now, **Who** becomes concerned with the fates of individuals rather than embracing hard science fiction's concern with the universal themes of progress or justice.'[114]

The Character of British Cinema

If *The Movie* was to have a truly British flavour, it needed to have been influenced not only by the original series of **Doctor Who**, but by British film and television as a whole. But what exactly is meant by British cinema? Defining the term is a political act in itself, one that has been a subject of much debate since the 1930s. Blockbuster movies such as the **Harry Potter** series, whilst filmed in England and utilising largely British personnel, are not commonly seen as being British products. The distinction between American and British movies is not always clear cut. Since the end of the Second World War, the British movie scene has been replete with cross-continental co-productions and with independent British movie makers who

---

[113] Wright, 'Expatriate, Expatriate', p139.
[114] Decker, Kevin, *Who Is Who: The Philosophy of Doctor Who*, p16.

have utilised Hollywood genres and techniques.

The British Film Institute commissioned a study aimed at identifying those key topics, value and qualities that moviegoers would identify as hallmarks of British cinema[115]. They arrived at eight recurring themes:

- **Small-Time Criminals.** British crime films are most often centred on the amateur criminal; opportunists and would-be villains who typically overreach themselves.

  Chang Lee has the potential to fit into this category, but without a backstory to provide motivation for his actions and to elicit sympathy from the viewers, he is effectively reduced to a mindless and ineffective henchman of the Master.

- **From the Everyman to the Eccentric.** After specialising in heroes who were ordinary people placed in an extraordinary setting, often for comic effect, British film turned to the non-conformist fashion rebel for inspiration.

  The Doctor, as we have seen, is a British eccentric, but one largely mediated through American views of Britishness. The script does not allow for his rebelliousness to be evidenced, and there are insufficient clues that this Doctor could position himself against the status quo. The narrative eschews the idealisation of the

---

[115] Narval Media, Birkbeck College and Media Consulting Group, 'Stories We Tell Ourselves: The Cultural Impact of UK Film, 1946-2006'.

everyman – Grace, for instance, is an exceptional surgeon. The Doctor tells one minor character, Gareth, that one day he will be important, implying that extraordinariness has to be earned. His fondness for namedropping implies he prefers to mix it with the movers and shakers of history, science and medicine. The 'unsung hero' trope is absent.

- **Qualified Victory.** The British hero is rarely allowed to revel in his triumph, tinged as it so often is with a sense of irony or disenchantment.

  There is no downside to the Doctor's triumph. *The Movie* is relentlessly optimistic, with characters even coming back from the dead. The Doctor readily accepts his hybridity and there is no pain or sense of loss as he leaves Grace behind at the end.

- **Shaken, Stirred and Undead.** Despite its 'Brit Grit' reputation for social realism (e.g. *Brassed Off* (1996), *The Full Monty* (1997)), there are a healthy number of fantastical protagonists in British cinema, from the magical (Harry Potter) to the super-heroic (James Bond).

  The Doctor is a romantic, fantastical hero, extraordinary both on account of his alien physiognomy and his enhanced abilities. Specifically he is likened to both Frankenstein and Christ.

- **Youthful Ambition.** The UK film industry has often played a key role in revolutionary youth movements, though its rebels will often get their comeuppance or settle for a quiet life.

This is another feature of British cinema that could have been present in the characterisation of Chang Lee, but is largely undone by his functional, plot-driven role. The eighth Doctor is younger than some, and he does at least appear to be enjoying the thrill of riding the bike and breaking the law in the process.

- **Backlight on the Present**. British produced period dramas are often used as morality tales for contemporary life.

Despite the Doctor having a time machine at his disposal, *The Movie* is entirely set in the near future.

- **Sex Please – We're British**. Contrary to the nation's reputation for prudishness, British cinema has frequently tackled controversial sexual and gender issues.

The eighth Doctor is far from prudish, and his sexuality is both owned and acted upon at a level appropriate to the target audience. Generally speaking the script plays it safe, reserving controversy to fan debates.

- **History from Beneath**. Whilst monarchy and the aristocracy are still popular subjects for British movies, there is a strand of film in which authority figures are subverted, or in which history is told from the bottom up, taking the perspective of a hitherto unknown or overlooked character[116]. An important rider to this category is that despite the assumption that Britain is

---

[116] Narval Media et al, 'Stories We Tell Ourselves', p18.

obsessed with its heritage, the vast majority of British movies are in fact set in the present day.

The Doctor's station on Gallifrey is not discussed, so there is no allegorical treatment of rank and privilege. The resolution of the threat by going back in time means that neither 'Amazing Grace' nor the street kid Chang Lee can take any credit for changing the course of history. The Doctor's habit of namedropping supports the official narratives, even with his 'revelation' that Puccini did not finish his opera.

When compared then to the hallmarks of British cinema, most of the features are either missing or barely present in *The Movie*. It is the character of the Doctor who is the primary mediator of Britishness.

Films that challenge contemporary cultural values account for the most recognisably British of titles, suggesting that whatever combination of the above themes is featured, the most memorable films are those which serve as vehicles for social and attitudinal reform[117]. Conservative films which mirror societal values have less immediate social impact, but will often continue to be popular over a longer period of time.

The BBC's television output, certainly during the early years of **Doctor Who**, was like the movies more than simply a mirror of the thoughts of the day. Funded by the taxpayer and with the government remit of being a public service broadcaster, that voice of resistance could not be quite as unabashed as it was for independent movie-makers. Danny Nicol convincingly argues that there is a

---

[117] Narval Media et al, 'Stories We Tell Ourselves', p16.

subtext of revolt underpinning **Doctor Who**[118]. This would explain the contradictions inherent in the series whereby the Doctor can be interpreted as both a revolutionary, anti-establishment figure, and a traditionalist defender of the status quo (and would make perfect sense of the BBC's failure to detect the political undertones to *The Happiness Patrol*, for instance).

The Virgin **New Adventures**, set up to be an official continuation of the seventh Doctor's adventures after *Survival*, had certainly pushed **Doctor Who** towards a greater level of realism and socio-political commentary, reflecting the trends of British film and television. In 2001 Russell T Davies recalled his experiences of reading the **New Adventure** *Timewyrm: Revelation* (1991) for the first time:

> 'Paul bloody Cornell gave us **Doctor Who**, but he made it real. I mean, real people, laid bare, exposing all their anger, passion and, dammit, nobility. People with histories and hopes and flaws, existing in a world where Chad Boyle, the school bully, is more terrifying than some super-evil Timewyrm.'[119]

The Movie is vastly different in that respect – after they have served their purpose and shot the Doctor, Chang Lee's pursuers completely disappear. Lee lacks any believable emotions, whether anger towards society or loyalty towards his fellow gang members. Despite the launch of eighth Doctor novel, audio and comic ranges, the movie remains a class apart. Some have even argued that the tie-in

---

[118] Utilising James Scott's theory of hidden transcripts (Nicol, *A British Alien*, p263). Since the BBC are obligated to be politically impartial such messages have to be codified.
[119] Quoted in Martin, 'Who Do We Think We Are?'

material had gone out of its way to depart from it:

> 'the **Doctor Who** spin-off world, being an outlet for fan
> creativity, cannibalised the TV Movie, remoulding the eighth
> Doctor into the characterisation they wanted him to have and
> – perhaps – what they though it should have been from the
> beginning.'[120]

In fairness, the failure to secure a licencing deal to use the characters
of Grace Holloway and Chang Lee did not help, but regular Virgin
Books writers such as Lance Parkin were less than complimentary
about *The Movie*, and the agenda to carve their own path was hardly
disguised:

> 'I'm not keen on Paul McGann's portrayal of the character in
> the TV Movie [...] I much preferred the one he talked about in
> interviews – one who's more like Gary Oldman in *Dracula* –
> this ancient, vampiric thing pretending to be a young man to
> impress birds. I don't want to take the credit for it, because I
> think a lot of people reached the same conclusions I did
> independently, but the Doctor in the [BBC Books] **Eighth
> Doctor Adventures** was far more like the Doctor in *The Dying
> Days* than the Doctor in *The Movie*.'[121]

The different ideology behind *The Movie* and the books and audios
is perhaps best illustrated by BBC Books' stipulation to Gary Russell
that the novelisation must steer clear of adult themes. The
opportunity to develop some of the barely-touched social

---

[120] Gulyas, Aaron, 'Don't Call it a Comeback', in Leitch, Gillian, ed,
Doctor Who in Time and Space, p55.
[121] Berry, Dan, 'Lance Parkin Interview (Part 1).'

dimensions to *The Movie*, such as Chang Lee's gang background, or to make the Master's degeneration as graphic as it had originally been intended, was therefore denied[122].

Whilst grittiness is seen as a defining factor for British movies, the Aardman animation, *Wallace and Gromit: The Curse of the Were-Rabbit* (2005) topped a 2011 BFI viewers' poll of which movie best represented Britishness. The authors of the report conclude that:

> 'if not displaying the grittiness that for many was one defining factor of Britishness, [*The Curse of the Were-Rabbit*] certainly eschews glitz and glamour in plot and scenario in favour of a more down-to-earth picture of life (no superhero saving the world, instead the rescue of a local vegetable show). It can also be taken as a type study of quirky British humour.'[123]

That same report notes that big budget and elaborate special effects can make a movie seem less British. Only 1% of respondents considered the special effects of a movie to be its most memorable feature. It goes on to conclude that the successful British film is most often grounded in a strong sense of place (whether in the UK or abroad), is laced with dark or quirky humour, stars British actors, tackles social issues or personal journeys with authenticity, and has the capacity to be both escapist and thought-provoking.

When viewed against the above criteria, we can clearly see why there is such debate about the national identity of **Doctor Who** in

---

[122] The book was to be aimed at 13-year-olds, rather than 17-year-olds as had been the case with the **New Adventures** (Segal with Russell, *Regeneration*, p152).

[123] Northern Alliance, Ipsos MediaCT, 'Opening Our Eyes: How Film Contributes to the Culture of the UK', p46.

The Movie. The movie certainly ticks the box of being well grounded in its San Francisco setting, and yet the BBC limited the degree of realism, particularly by requesting that the scenes in the hospital be cut down. It is also apparent that, whilst humour plays a key role, the BBC's dislike for 1980s **Doctor Who** took away much of the satire. The casting of Paul McGann as the Doctor maintains the character's role as the representative of Britain on the global stage, but his lack of critical engagement, for instance with Chang Lee's gang culture, reduces him to a foppish stereotype. The emotional impact of the Doctor's self-discovery is somewhat diminished by the suppression of the half-human story, and whilst *The Movie* would score highly on the escapist front, the messages it conveys are hardly deep or relatable.

WHO AM I? REIMAGINING THE DOCTOR FOR A NEW AUDIENCE

In order to make a new Doctor relatable to its core audience, the writers, directors and producers have always made explicit the similarities and differences between the new incumbent and his or her predecessors, both in the marketing and the story itself. Sometimes the final run of a Doctor will also be used to foreshadow what changes the viewers can expect (most notably the hints at the Doctor's gender change in series 10). What sets *The Movie* apart from other debut Doctor episodes is the very different art of writing an existing character for a new audience. The focus here is not on the change of actor, but on the change of viewers. To avoid alienating the committed fanbase, who will after all be as important in marketing the series as official trailers and media appearances, at the most basic level there are nods to past Doctors. Whilst such continuity might be seen as important to the fans, it plays a minimal role in the movie, as evidenced by the token appearance of the Daleks:

> 'The reduction of the Daleks from cultural icon and powerful metaphor for totalitarian authority to a gaggle of off screen, apolitical voices is emblematic of the irrelevance of most "concessions" to continuity.'[124]

The whole opening scene, whilst intended to establish continuity from the outset, throws up a number of inconsistencies and departures, from the idea that the Daleks would hold a formal trial against an alien, to the implication that they would be happy to let

---

[124] Wright, 'Expatriate, Expatriate', p133.

the Doctor take the Master's remains back to Gallifrey. A slight adjustment to the narration script could easily have presented their actions as a trick to capture and exterminate their greatest enemy, with the Doctor in typical fashion thwarting their plan. The Daleks' iconic role in the series as the Doctor's archenemy is however, deliberately masked in order not to detract from the archetypal struggle between the two Time Lords. Such peculiarities are allowed to stand, despite all the offscreen pandering to the fanbase, because it is the new audience that sets the agenda. It was a gamble that largely paid off, for as our survey demonstrates the discontinuities with the Daleks were overlooked, with their very mention enough to please most fans of the series. Continuity is established, says Gulyas, but with errors and additions[125].

Since the Doctor is scripted as if from scratch, rather than draw comparisons with past iterations of the character the makers of *The Movie* use analogies from outside the **Doctor Who** universe. The contrast between the seventh Doctor and the eighth has only metatextual significance insofar as it encapsulates a kind of Old Testament-New Testament break to please those in the BBC who believed that the show had lost its way. For the uninitiated, McCoy's role is simply to establish the Doctor's ability to regenerate. His character is therefore intentionally ill-defined. The eighth Doctor emerges not as the seventh reborn or reimagined, but as Frankenstein and his monster, Jesus Christ, Batman, the Beast in Beauty and the Beast, Lord Byron and Wild Bill Hickok. To ensure that *The Movie* is brought into the fold and not sidelined as an alternative version like the Cushing movies, it will be necessary to see whether

---

[125] Gulyas, 'Don't Call it a Comeback', p51.

those models could equally apply to other Doctors.

Frankenstein and his Monster

In the script, Matthew Jacobs did not specify which film the morgue attendant Pete was watching while the Doctor regenerated. When first introduced, Jacobs specifies only that it was a black and white picture. It is not until the risen Doctor begins to knock on the door of his 'body room' that the viewers are directed to see that Pete has been watching a horror movie[126]. This whole scene is heavily signposted as a meta-reference to the audience witnessing the resurrection of a long-running TV series, one that had begun before the invention of colour TV. There is an added layer of resonance, given that the movie selected by Sax was the forerunner to a multitude of screen versions of *Frankenstein*[127]. The choice is perfectly in keeping with Segal's efforts to be mindful of the roots of **Doctor Who**, and of William Hartnell as the original.

The fact that Pete is watching a horror movie may well be an artefact of the Halloween setting of Jacobs' earlier drafts, but after re-dating the story to the end of the millennium, the movie could have been replaced with a Christmas one, or presented as a character trait for Pete on the basic assumption that a person who wanted to work in a morgue might also be attracted to the dark and the gruesome. Instead Sax uses *Frankenstein* (1931) as an effective analogy for the events that are occurring behind Pete. James Whale's monster is neatly analogous with the Doctor's unnatural rebirth, and comes

---

[126] Jacobs, *The Script of the Film*, p33.
[127] Though frequently celebrated as the original *Frankenstein* screen adaptation, it was preceded by the silent movies *Frankenstein* (1910) and *Life Without Soul* (1915).

with the added advantage of being a hugely iconic and well-known figure.

Jacobs recalls that the Frankenstein motif was also chosen to 'puncture' the Christlike allusions of the resurrected Time Lord[128]. Geoffrey Sax cut directly from the animating of Frankenstein's monster to the Doctor's regeneration, and added into the mix an additional scene of the Doctor seeing the newly risen monster on the screen, making it less about Pete and his tastes and more about the Doctor's monstrous awakening[129]. We are prompted to wonder whether the Doctor sees himself as a monster. He has emerged with a perfect face – unbloodied and unstressed, unlike that of a newborn baby – but does his ability to return from the dead with a completely new body make him a monster by default? To add to the fear that his resurrection is unnatural and potentially even an abomination, we later see the macabre image of a child's baby doll with its head twisted 180 degrees.

Prior to *The Movie* the most explicit reference to Frankenstein in

---

[128] More in reference to Shelley's novel with its comparative lack of the supernatural and the religious than the Whale movies in which the creature was increasingly turned into a Christlike figure (e.g. *Bride of Frankenstein* (1934)).

[129] This scene appears to have been an even later development from the decision to use James Whale's *Frankenstein*. The novelisation has the Doctor spotting Tom and Jerry (or possibly Itchy and Scratchy) on the TV, as some time after his regeneration he visits the morgue to retrace his steps (Russell, *The Novel of the Film*, p62). Russell uses the Doctor's reaction to highlight his non-violence. The decision to use *Frankenstein* to secularise the otherwise overly religious connotations of the Doctor's resurrection may then have been a revision made after realising the extent of the Christ allusions.

televised **Doctor Who** is 'Journey Into Terror' (*The Chase* episode 4, 1965)[130]. Unbeknown to the Doctor and his companions, their efforts to escape the Daleks have taken them forward in time to (somewhat ironically) 1996. Britain in the 60s clearly had unrealistic expectations about the speed of technological development, since the Frankenstein's monster they encounter in 1996 is a highly advanced robot inside a theme park attraction, conveniently indestructible and super-strong for when the Daleks arrive (and also advanced enough to change his own costume). The influence of James Whale's movie on the popular look of the monster is reflected in the creature's design, making the endurance of this iconic figure the only thing the episode correctly predicted about 1996.

Since his cartoon-like appearance in *The Chase*, the creature has occasionally been a dark inspiration for the show's villains and beasts (e.g. *The Brain of Morbius*, *Black Orchid* (1982), and *Deep Breath* (2014)), but *The Movie* is unique in drawing out the parallels with the Doctor. The analogy is slightly obscured by the fact that the Doctor could also be likened to Victor (Henry) Frankenstein. He claims to be the agency behind his own resurrection, telling Grace 'I came back to life before your eyes, I held back death.'[131] Scholars of Shelley's novel would argue that there is a certain inevitability behind this conflation of Victor and his monster, and they are often sympathetic towards

---

[130] There are relatively few on-screen references compared to those in the tie-in audios and novels (which are mostly associated with the eighth Doctor, who even gets to have Mary Shelley as a companion).
[131] Presumably a reference to his brief awakening on the operating table, given that he regenerated alone, but nonetheless an indication that the ability to be resurrected is an inherent aspect of his Time Lord physiognomy.

the tendency to call the creation by the name of his creator. Harold Bloom, for instance, suggests that 'the monster and his creator are the antithetical halves of a single being.'[132] The relationship is more nuanced than, say, the one representing emotion and the other reason. Frankenstein's monster begins to think and talk like his creator, partly because he has been crafted in his maker's image but primarily because the two characters are inspired by the same figure – the ancient Prometheus as reimagined through the contemporary lens of Milton's Adam in *Paradise Lost*.

At the heart of Mary Shelley's novel is the Byronic juxtaposition of the human with the monstrous, internalised in Victor with his mixture of pride and regret at his achievement, and externalised in his creature as one who can commit the most heinous crimes and yet elicit sympathy for his plight. The monster is literally both man and beast, representing the duality of Frankenstein himself as hero and villain. If anything, both the human and the monstrous are exaggerated in the creature so that he ends up being the most human and the most alien character in the story.

It was the friendship between the Shelleys and Lord Byron that inspired Mary Shelley (then Mary Godwin) to write *Frankenstein: Or, the Modern Prometheus* (1818), after Byron had set his friends a challenge to come up with a ghost story. It cannot therefore be a coincidence that the predominant image of the eighth Doctor is that of the Byronic hero. The Frankenstein allusion seals the deal in that respect, and offers the clearest window into the darker shades of the romantic character, even if the story insists that like the Doctor we

---

[132] Bloom, Harold, *Bloom's Major Literary Characters: Frankenstein*, p2.

do not spend too much time looking into it.

Frankenstein's story taps into the Doctor's duality and helps to foster the paradoxical impression that the eighth Doctor is one of the most human and most alien of incarnations, a figure to be trusted and feared, reliable and unpredictable, passionate and cold – the kind of person you would be foolish to reject and equally foolish to follow. The Doctor is also presented as both a blast from the black-and-white past and the herald of a new dawn for the show, a legend as enduring as Shelley's modern Prometheus; old-fashioned and futuristic, belonging and not belonging to the here and now, as befitting a wanderer in time and space.

The *Frankenstein* parallels could also be a helpful framework for understanding the tension between the Doctor's conservatism and liberalism. The fall of Shelley's monster has been read by Robert Ryan as a cautionary tale about how the values of traditional Christianity ought to be preserved in the face of a relentless humanism, but it is also an exposé of the religion's impotence[133]. According to Ryan, Shelley yearns nostalgically for a Christianity that will ironically humanise those around her whose ultra-rationalistic approach had brought a coldness in the face of life's inscrutable sufferings. The monster's faith devastatingly brings an awareness of sin without any hope of redemption. The novel then is resolutely against any forms of ideology, but only on the grounds that the people espousing such views are flawed and broken. Frankenstein's monster is a 'disconnected Christian whose faith can bring no hope,'[134] and

---

[133] Ryan, Robert, 'Mary Shelley's Christian Monster', *The Wordsworth Circle* 19:3.

[134] Ryan, 'Mary Shelley's Christian Monster', p153.

Frankenstein himself, as a metaphor for her father William Godwin, is satirised in the novel for his personality flaws rather than for his beliefs.

Godwin was relentlessly demonised by traditionalists, and his utopian quest satirised in numerous monster narratives[135]. The brilliance of Shelley's work is that it is a parody of such satires and yet also one of their most effective examples. In a delicious act of irony, Shelley dedicated later editions of 'The Modern Prometheus' to her father, thus helping to conceal the book's counternarrative behind a more explicit debunking of the monster's Christianity. *Frankenstein* is a morality tale without a resolution. It is concerned with deeply theological issues such as the nature of humanity and of good and evil, but it leaves unanswered the key existential question, namely what, if anything, sets us apart from the material world?

The Doctor, like Frankenstein and his monster, is a fictional character continuously caught in a liminal position between the dialectics of conservatism and radicalism, old-fashioned and post-modern, rationality and emotion, science and magic, creator and creation, promiscuity and abstinence, compliance and anarchy, the grotesque and the beautiful, good and evil, angel and devil, alien and familiar, superhuman and subhuman. Properly speaking, none of these dialectics can be truly reconciled without one side taking ownership of the other. *The Movie* is an enactment of the triumph of the conservative over the liberal, but by seeing the Doctor through the mirror of Frankenstein and his monster, a counternarrative can be

---

[135] See Sterrenburg, Lee, 'Mary Shelley's Monster: Politics and Psyche in *Frankenstein*', in Levine, George, and UC Knoepflmacher, eds, *The Endurance of 'Frankenstein': Essays on Mary Shelley's Novel*.

read that subverts the ideologies of the series and its writers. In this case, **Doctor Who** and its 'believers', rather than Christianity or Godwinianism, are the objects of parody. In many respects, the struggles involved in the making of *The Movie* were struggles against the monster that **Doctor Who** (itself a creation) had created.

Jesus Christ Super Time Lord

When drawing out the Christlikeness of the Doctor, the theological complexities of Christology, with its highly-charged historical debates over the relationship between the divinity and humanity of Jesus, tend to be conveniently overlooked in favour of a basic Sunday School equation of the man from Palestine with God. The Doctor is therefore primarily associated with a highly mythologised version of Jesus whose image is derived from Western paintings and whose character is defined by Victorian sensibilities. This Jesus is apolitical, white and puritanical – the head of a highly structured and authoritarian institution rather than the leader of a chaotic band of mismatched social rebels and outcasts. Of course, both versions of Christ are ideologically-driven constructs made from the flimsiest pieces of historical evidence and the wildest feats of conjecture, and yet they are powerful enough to inspire wars and revolutions, the rising up of empires and their downfalls.

The Christlikeness of the eighth Doctor has been used as evidence for a conservatism in *The Movie* that is at sharp odds from the Wellsian British Time Lord who promoted responsible cultural perspectivism and a post-Empire liberal agenda of inclusivity and tolerance. The struggle between the Doctor and the Master is removed from any personal history and context and firmly placed on a spiritual plane. Even science and technology are turned into religious metaphors, from the cross-shaped beryllium chip to the contraption that the Master places on the Doctor's head, leading Peter Wright to conclude 'what was once a secular struggle between two Time Lords is now a spiritual conflict for souls, futures and [...] states of grace.'[136] Wright argues that this is a departure from both the rationalism and the liberalism of the original series. The Doctor's acts of salvation and liberation, once politically motivated, are now firmly bound up with his need to save himself, leading to an eighth Doctor who is 'a politically sanitised version of the Christian saviour whose love for humanity is boundless.'[137] Wright proposes that the reason for such a dramatic shift is to make the series and the character more palatable for the Fox audience.

In some ways Wright's point is understated. The Doctor calls to mind Robert Powell's blue-eyed **Jesus of Nazareth** (1977). He even has his very own walking-on-water moments, from the 'miraculous' walking through glass, to the literal crossing of the stepping stones in his final scene with Grace. The mixed metaphor of the crown of nails doubles up the references to the crucifixion to drum home the point. Grace's nickname, which in earlier drafts evokes the glamour of Hollywood (Grace Kelly), becomes 'Amazing Grace', an evangelical hymn played at many a Billy Graham crusade as part of the call to conversion. Grace's journey is that of a proselyte as she abandons the Hollywood dream and her materialistic lifestyle to follow the Doctor. She ends up losing everything, but finding herself in the process – 'I know who I am.' Far from being a prototype for a more enlightened female companion, she has effectively traded in her expertise for ignorance,

---

[136] Wright, 'Expatriate, Expatriate', p138.
[137] Wright, 'Expatriate, Expatriate', p140.

and knowledge for blind faith, killing the Doctor with her surgical skills but then saving the day through sheer luck. Just as Christianity sets itself in opposition to other faiths and creeds, so too the way of the Doctor is presented as the only true path to enlightenment. Wealth is one of the opposing false gods, exploited to great effect by the Master in his temptation of Lee. Time itself is another, a lesser power that is worshipped by humanity (explicitly so by Professor Wagg[138], but notice too, the sheer number of clocks that appear throughout the movie). The Doctor is the literal Lord of Time as symbolised by his huge clock collection. Time itself is subjugated to him as he runs around giving spoilers, only to warn Grace that such a gift is reserved for him[139].

The Christological analogies in *The Movie* however, fail at the most critical of junctures. Despite the Master being clearly modelled on Satan (as we will see shortly), at no point does he act as a tempter to the Doctor; instead his prey is Chang Lee. Grace too fails to distract the Doctor from his role, with no hint of regret on his part as he turns down the opportunity to stay on Earth with her. The Doctor's journey does not include an analogous baptism, wilderness sojourn, transfiguration or Gethsemane moment. Without such markers the allusions to Christ cannot be described as narrative-defining.

---

[138] Less so in the published script, which lacks the incantation. There is a hint of parody here, calling to mind similar acts of religious mumbo-jumbo in the original series.
[139] With the new millennium on the horizon, there was an unprecedented level of interest in how we measure time. In one of his final public appearances, shortly before *The Movie* aired, as part of the BBC's science week Jon Pertwee visited the National Physical Laboratory, the home of the world's first atomic clock since 1955.

In the 21st-century series the Doctor is frequently likened to Christ in his role as a messianic figure, and as a result those biblical markers are established at various points. Several characters and organisations play the role of John the Baptist in both preparing the way and commissioning him for his role as defender of the Earth and saviour of worlds. The 11th Doctor goes through his own wilderness experience following the loss of Amy and Rory in *The Snowmen* (2012). The 10th Doctor ascends borne by angels in *Voyage of the Damned* (2007) before being literally transfigured in *Last of the Time Lords* (2008), and the 12th Doctor spends a whole series fighting against his 'calling'. Missy's goals are also more in line with the biblical stories than are the Roberts Master's. She tempts the Doctor to renounce his ethical and missiological stands, offering him a Cyber-army and using Clara as a temptress rather than her prey. The Doctor's companions in the 21st-century series are as much a hindrance as a help, often distracting him and causing him to question his calling.

For *The Movie* the Doctor's Christlikeness is more an ontological reality than it is a mission. Like Christ he is both fully human and fully alien. His mother is human and his father the equivalent of a god. He is therefore able to work miracles but also perform conjuring tricks. This focus on the Doctor remembering who he is and finding his place again, both of and not of this world, should be sufficient explanation for the lack of politics and social commentary. To suggest an American audience would not be ready for a more libertarian Doctor patronises them. To argue that the eighth Doctor is an establishment figure overlooks Philip Segal's very clear antihero guidelines to Jacobs and the channelling of other characters, most notably Frankenstein, Batman and Byron. But equally, to posit that in the original series the Doctor is following a supposed liberal agenda of the BBC, conveniently forgets the numerous examples to the contrary.

The Dark Knight

The late journalist John Diamond, reviewing the movie for *The New Statesman*, was less than enthused by what he saw as a move away from the fantastical, superheroic nature of the Doctor: 'Now we have an eighth Dr Who and, like the new Batman, he lives in the real world. Or, rather, the flickering half-light which passes for the real world in this sort of gothic romp.'[140] Bemoaning the modern and rather grown-up trend of pouring increasingly heavy dollops of pathos and angst into our most beloved comic-book superheroes, he detected a similar tendency to psychoanalyse the Doctor in *The Movie*. Observing how the production riffs on numerous blockbuster movies, including *Alien* (1979) and *The Terminator* (1984), he singles out the Tim Burton's **Batman** movies (beginning with *Batman* (1989)) as the biggest influence.

In truth, judging from the critical reaction to the darker elements of *Batman Returns* (1992) and the resultant tonal shift in *Batman Forever* (1995), in which director Joel Schumacher tried and ultimately failed to draw equal inspiration from the Burton movies and the 60s series, there was a mood to return to the more optimistic feel of the first Richard Donner **Superman** movies. Like Schumacher, Segal was attempting to reconcile two quite different visions of his source material. Channelling the original series whilst at the same

---

[140] Diamond, John, 'Doctor Why?' *The New Statesman*, 31 May 1996, p35.

time framing it in the modern sensibilities of the likes of Tim Burton was always going to provoke criticisms from both traditionalist and modernist wings. Stylistically, the gothic feel, whilst adding darker shades to the hero, does not sit comfortably with the British gentleman and his jelly babies. The juxtaposition of the gothic and comedy worked for Tom Baker in the 70s because the nature of his alienness suggested that he was weighed down by burdens and knowledge beyond our understanding, whereas for the eighth Doctor alienness is used to signify the very opposite – a naïve, charming and innocent faith. It's no coincidence that the jelly babies were dropped for Peter Davison's what-you-see-is-what-you-get Doctor. He could be as moody and mysterious as the best of them, but such moments always felt superficial and easily passed like a child having a sulk.

That we are meant to view *The Movie* through the expectations of a Batman movie is largely betrayed by the design of the TARDIS, complete with its very own bats. This is the closest the TARDIS has ever been to a Batcave and all it signifies about its owner being a loner, set apart and emotionally guarded. The score and cinematography also share much in common with the Burton **Batman** movies. San Francisco can be likened to Gotham City with the night time panorama (the fictional city is commonly depicted as New York at night, compared to Superman's Metropolis as New York by day) and with the contrast between the gangland violence of Chinatown and the wealth on display at the ITAR reception. The Doctor himself, however, lacks the dangerous qualities that are inherent in the vigilante masked hero. The dynamic between the Doctor and Grace carries a distinct vibe of **Lois and Clark: The New Adventures of Superman** (1993-1997), which further distances him from the Caped Crusader at his darkest.

But *The Movie* does hold far more in common with **Batman Forever**, with its echoes of the very different, tongue-in-cheek 1960s **Batman** series (1966-68). The frozen fate of the security guards is straight out of the 60s Batman stable, as is the campness of the Master. The San Francisco of 1999 is not quite the decayed den of corruption and criminality that Gotham became in the 70s comics (though there are echoes of it in the abandoned hospital ward) and the police are presented as clueless rather than powerless or corrupt. Jacobs wanted instead to convey a more optimistic version of his adopted city, one with increased diversity[141]. The movie's climax follows the pattern of the Caped Crusader being placed in a deadly trap by his nemesis and needing his gadgets and partner to turn the tables on the villain.

In the original series, whilst there are a couple of odd incidental references to Batman (e.g. Ace's earring, and the Doctor's toy Batmobile in *The Talons of Weng Chiang* (1977)), there is only one scene of note that compares and contrasts the Doctor directly with the superhero. The third Doctor responds with sarcasm when Greg Sutton is underwhelmed by the Heath Robinson appearance of the TARDIS console (*Inferno* (1970)):

SUTTON

I thought it would be a bit more impressive than that.

DOCTOR

What did you expect? Some kind of space rocket with Batman

---

[141] See Appendix 2.

at the controls?[142]

In distancing himself from unrealistic comic-book heroes and technology, the Doctor is acting as a spokesperson for the perceived distinctiveness of British fantasy and **Doctor Who** in particular (it is no coincidence that Sutton is Australian). In *The Mind Robber* (1968) the Doctor comes face to face with an in-universe comic book hero, the Karkus. The representative superhero from Zoe's era comes complete with unrealistic weapons and a preference for brawn over brain, but ends up stripped of his anti-molecular ray gun and subservient to the Doctor and his companions. Although Zoe's martial arts skills beat him into submission, the Karkus' fate is a clear statement about the superiority of British sci-fi over its foreign equivalents (the Karkus is given a German accent). Whilst the Doctor becomes the Karkus, literally pretending to be him by wearing his cape and later using the superhero's un-Doctor-like methods against the Master of Fiction's soldiers, the absurdity of the situation calls for absurdly comic-book like resolutions.

The Doctor can only use the anti-molecular ray gun to help destroy a fictional construct. As he and the Master of Fiction, controlled by the supercomputer, continue to up the stakes in their use of the fictional characters, the Doctor draws the line at writing the death of the only real character in the world, other than his friends. The Master of the Land of Fiction is saved despite Jamie's protests, and with a polite Britishness the Doctor asks, 'Are you all right, sir?'[143] Ultimately the Doctor eschews the Karkus' methods, the implication being that such a character is no use in the real world. The Doctor is contrasted with

---

[142] *Inferno* episode 6.
[143] *The Mind Robber* episode 5.

a superhero, lacking either avenging motives or a desire to enforce the law. He is a hero who brings liberation rather than retribution.

In the 21st-century series, especially under Steven Moffat's stewardship, the question of what kind of hero the Doctor is plays a defining role. The American superhero is one of a number of hero types to which the Doctor is compared. *The Return of Doctor Mysterio* (2016) begins with the Doctor hanging Batman-like outside Grant's bedroom window. The Doctor is decidedly anti-American throughout, at one point noting 'Brains with minds of their own? No one will believe that. This is America.' He is also iconoclastic and dismissive when it comes to numerous comic-book tropes, such as his impatience with the constant teasing of the Ghost's identity reveals. Despite this, the episode was written as a homage to the early **Superman** movies, a move away from the grittiness of contemporary superhero treatments to a more innocent, more optimistic time[144]. The Doctor even adopts some of the clichés himself: 'With great power comes great responsibility.' But the superhero's journey, whilst replete with all the expected story elements, is not the Doctor's.

The Doctor is set apart as a different kind of hero altogether, one who in the words of Nardole is brave and silly, one who by his own admission is making it up as he goes. Ironically, the story's stereotypical superhero is born out of the Doctor's poor judgement, naivety and carelessness. Despite all his best efforts the Doctor is powerless to stop Grant using his powers. The Doctor believes, somewhat hypocritically, that such abilities are not of this world and

---

[144] Mulkern, Patrick, 'Steven Moffat Reveals (Almost) All about the Doctor Who Christmas Special'.

therefore should never be used. The Time Lord might arrogantly present himself as the great defender of the human race, but Nardole gets to the nub of it when he explains that the Doctor's mission is nothing more than a diversion from his loss of River Song. In that respect there is a deep seated underlying tragedy and pain at work that resembles that of Bruce Wayne following the death of his parents. If there is a superhero analogy to be drawn between 'Doctor Mysterio' and the comic books then it is indeed Batman, with Grant playing the contrasting Superman.

This kind of psychological motivation is one that *The Movie* utterly avoids, despite the fertile ground of the half-human revelation. The Doctor is Batman only in appearances, and yet it could be reasonably argued that by attaching superhero motifs to the Doctor *The Movie* provides a bridge between the 20th and the 21st-century series, between the Doctor being antithetical to traditional comic-book characters and being a British version of the American superhero. The second Doctor is dismissive of comics, implying he has better things to do with his time, whereas the 12th Doctor claims, albeit dubiously, to be an expert in their finer points. He might set himself up as the dark overlord, looking down on the Earth as its protector from a position of transcendence and omniscience, but like the third Doctor, his gadgets are considered cheap, this time even from a young boy's perspective[145]. A similar observation is made by Grace when she calls the TARDIS console 'pretty low-tech'. Aside from the TARDIS, in *The Movie* the Doctor is gadget-free, a point he bemoans

---

[145] Another sideswipe against the unenlightened criticism of **Doctor Who** as a low-budget British series that looks to ape a superior American product.

whilst missing his sonic screwdriver, which unlike the TARDIS set has not undergone an upgrade. Not only does it look cheap, but it also fails spectacularly to do the one job asked of it in *The Movie* – securing the Master's remains in the casket.

The Beast

Steven Moffat's run as executive producer is likely to be remembered as the 'fairytale' era, a convenient way of distinguishing it from the 'soap opera' approach of Russell T Davies. Both labels are over-simplifications and the supposed gulf between the styles and interests of two showrunners is a fan invention. That said, the fantastical tone for series 5 was firmly set with the 'Alice down the rabbit hole' trailer, and in numerous interviews Moffat was keen to emphasise the links between **Doctor Who** and the fairytale[146]. Clarifying his oft-quoted 'dark fairytale' description of the series, Moffat admitted that the word 'dark' was redundant. Traditional fairytales have a dark quality to them as they twist the familiar, giving them an alien and eerie quality, and Moffat was keen to draw out the hidden horrors lurking behind the everyday:

> 'fairytales of old would use the real world around them of forests and villages, and make them dark and mysterious and reveal dangers in the shadows, so **Doctor Who** does that at its best. Because a lot of **Doctor Who** takes the real-life world around you and twists it a bit.'[147]

In setting out his stall, Moffat was keen to highlight what he saw as

---

[146] See Arnold, Jon, *The Black Archive #19: The Eleventh Hour* pp61-70.

[147] Anders, Charlie, '**Doctor Who**'s Steven Moffat: the io9 Interview.'

the essence of **Doctor Who**. The series might have the power of regeneration running through its bones, but it retains a thematic core that has more in common with the fairytale than science-fiction. Documentation from the prehistory of the show reveals just how anxious the early-60s BBC were to avoid their new show being labelled as 'hard science fiction'. There was a firm belief that the audience would be not ready for such a genre. They were also conscious of the fact that they would lack both the budgets and the calibre of writers to do the genre justice. However, CE 'Bunny' Webber was also keen to avoid the show being labelled as 'fantasy'. The characters had to be believable and their experiences credible. The Doctor's time machine was an excellent case in point:

> 'We are in danger of science fiction or fairytale labelling. If it is a transparent plastic bubble we are with all the low-grade space fiction of cartoon strip and soap opera. If we scotch this by positing something humdrum, say passing through some common object in (the) street such as a night watchman's shelter to arrive inside a marvellous contrivance of quivering electronics then we simply have a version of the dear old Magic door.'[148]

Despite these cautionary words, by taking the 'magic door' approach to even greater extremes with the TARDIS being bigger on the inside, **Doctor Who** was positioning itself from the outset as a modern-day fairytale. It quickly became apparent that the show had to be both –

---

[148] Quoted in Butler, David, 'How to Pilot a TARDIS: Audience, Science Fiction and the Fantastic in **Doctor Who**', in Butler, David, ed, *Time and Relative Dissertations in Space: Critical Perspectives on Doctor Who*, p21.

science fiction was the only way to lend credibility to the otherwise impossible, and the fantastic added a sense of mystery and ensured that writers would not be bound or judged by the limits of scientific knowledge.

David Butler favourably compares *An Unearthly Child* (1963) to *The Movie*, arguing that the former is shrouded in mystery whilst the latter is at pains to explain everything from the outset. Pointing out the difference between Barbara and Grace's reactions to the TARDIS interior, he suggests that the sense of wonder is undone by Grace's matter-of-fact response. Overlooking both the fact that Grace's 'knowledge' is a sign that she has been possessed by the Master, and Chang Lee's earlier more expected reaction, for Butler this is another case of the producers spoon-feeding the audience. He concludes that the movie takes a fairytale approach of using formulaic patterns framed by 'Once upon a time' and 'They all lived happily ever after.'[149] In so doing, it has moved away from the fantastic and towards the marvellous. If *An Unearthly Child* made the familiar strange, *The Movie* made the strange familiar. This may well account for Butler's research findings, in which first-time viewers responded more positively to *An Unearthly Child* than *The Movie*, but it is a somewhat disingenuous assessment given that *The Movie* was working with an existing mythology.

One casualty of Butler's unfavourable assessment of *The Movie* is John Debney's score. Compared to Norman Kay's low key, unpredictable eerie 1963 score, Debney's, in typical Hollywood fashion, follows the action with all the appropriate, obvious and overbearing emotional cues. A more considered interpretation

---

[149] Butler, 'How to Pilot a TARDIS', p28.

would be to see his work as a necessary tool for bringing **Doctor Who** into the mainstream. Debney guides the audience by channelling a number of familiar scores, including the theme tune for Disney's rendition of the classic French fairytale 'La Belle et la Bête', *Beauty and the Beast* (1991). Not only is the music in keeping with the consistent presentation of **Doctor Who** as a modern fairytale, in evoking one such tale in particular it presents the Doctor as a modern-day reimagining of the Beast.

In somewhat tongue-in-cheek fashion, the parallels between the Doctor and Disney's version of the Beast received some recent attention online when the *Radio Times* website shared a Reddit post speculating that the Beast could even be a Time Lord[150]. Indeed, it is quite plausible that the regeneration effect from Eccleston onwards was partly inspired by the yellow glow of the Beast as he regenerates back into the prince. *The Movie* of course takes a very different approach to the regeneration effect[151], and the parallels to *Beauty and the Beast* here are instead exclusively connected to the Doctor's relationship with Grace (though it is also interesting to note the clock and candle motifs inside the Doctor's equivalent of the Beast's palace, the TARDIS). Just as Belle makes the Beast human again, so too Grace restores the Doctor to the man he was before he regenerated.

Whilst the Disney movie reinforces a number of unfortunate stereotypes (parodied and reversed to great effect in *Shrek* (2001)),

---

[150] Doran, Sarah, 'This Fan Theory Has Convinced Us There's a Secret Time Lord Hiding in *Beauty and the Beast*.'
[151] Though there is a similar effect in *The Movie* as Grace and Chang Lee are brought back to life.

and does indeed reduce the fairytale to the predictable and the formulaic, more modern treatments of the story have drawn out the heroic, Byronic qualities of the original Beast[152]. The 1987 CBS fantasy romance series **Beauty and the Beast** was an unexpected hit, and was still fondly remembered in 1996. The mythic in the ordinary lies at the core of that show, both in the characters and the New York setting, and a similar tone is established here. Writer George RR Martin describes Vincent, the Beast, as 'an intellectual who loved words and stories and poems. He was not by that reason like a geek or a figure the other characters made fun of but was in fact a classic, Romantic, Byronic hero.'[153] Similarly, the Doctor of *The Movie* is a bookish lover of art and literature. Vincent literally saves Catherine Chandler and draws her into a world she never knew existed. Grace is saved metaphorically speaking from overly demanding men (her boss, her boyfriend) and begins to see the world through dimensions that her rationalist mind would initially deny. She is attracted to the Doctor because of his alienness. The Doctor's likeness to the Beast is less immediate, since in his case the monstrous is internal. He is the Beast turned inside out. His humanity is readily apparent with his good looks, whilst his alien and by association monstrous nature is revealed by his two hearts.

The Byronic Hero

We have seen how the Doctor is likened in *The Movie* to various legendary figures – a monster, a god, a superhero and a fairytale

---

[152] See for instance, Robert Carlyle's Rumpelstiltskin in **Once Upon a Time** (2011-18).
[153] Abramovitch, Seth, 'George RR Martin on Writing TV's *Beauty and the Beast*: "It Was Such a Smart Show".'

character, and contrary to Butler's critique the interplay between these overlapping but sometimes conflicting images provides exactly the level of mystery that makes both him and the series so hard to pin down. But all these character types do share one thing in common: they are all various manifestations of the Byronic hero type who in himself is a highly ambiguous figure. Arguably, the explicit association of the Doctor with Byron is the greatest contribution *The Movie* has made to **Doctor Who** lore, insofar as it offers a useful category for plotting continuity in difference.

The Romantic hero's main quest is to discover what it means to be fully human. In the late 18th century, with the Enlightenment's pursuit of the ideal society and its deification of reason having both been called into question, the time had come for the human race to look within rather than outside for value and meaning. This post-Enlightenment individualistic mind-set is reflected in the Doctor's own story[154]. He may be an alien, but in that respect he represents the sense of detachment that haunts the contemporary individual.

The Byronic hero is a particularly brash and iconoclastic variant of the 18th-century Romantic. Composites of both the real life Lord Bryon and his self-referential fictional characters, such rebels set themselves apart as 'Me against the world' and call others to join in the struggle:

> 'Bryon created heroes who embody the ultimate in individualism, self-sufficiency, ambition and aspiration, yet who are isolated, gloomy, unsatisfied, and dangerous to

---

[154] Decker, Kevin, 'The Ethics of the Last of the Time Lords' in Lewis, Courtlans, and Paula Smithka, eds, *Doctor Who and Philosophy*, p136.

themselves and others. In their autonomy, their insistence on defining their own moral code, and their superhuman abilities, they provide a vicarious antidote to their readers' own sense of helplessness and powerlessness in the face of institutional oppression.'[155]

Occupying a liminal space both in and not of the world, such characters are for the most part wanderers or exiles. In the Doctor's case, *The Movie* expresses this duality in terms of his half-human, half-Time Lord nature, but the series has depicted the Doctor as cut off from his own people right from the beginning. *The Movie* makes no reference to the Doctor's dislocation from his people, and 22 years on, the seemingly obvious link between homelessness and hybridity has still not been firmly established. The closest we come is in *Hell Bent* (2015), which despite apparently revealing the Doctor and Clara to be jointly the apocalyptic 'Hybrid' of Gallifreyan legend, leaves open the possibility that the Doctor is indeed half-human. Capaldi is the most obviously Byronic incarnation of the Doctor, and that dangerous aspect is no better expressed than in the series 9 finale and his efforts to bring Clara back from the dead.

The romantic lure of the Byronic hero is largely a consequence of his flamboyant and idiosyncratic behaviour[156]. A central paradox is that while he is a loner and sets himself up as deliberately aloof from others he is also able, through the sheer weight of his personality, to command a following. After Byron's death a personality cult rose up to immortalise him as an archetypical hero, consigning to history his

---

[155] Marin, Cristina, 'The Byronic Hero', *Language and Literature: European Landmarks of Identity* 4 (2), p82.
[156] The Byronic hero is typically male.

more unsavoury qualities.

The image most commonly associated with the Byronic hero is of the brooding and tortured soul who masks his pain behind a handsome exterior. The darker tones of the eighth Doctor are somewhat suppressed in *The Movie*, but they are not entirely absent. Grace suspects that he may have been the result of a genetic experiment. His 'blood' is so extraordinary she cannot even describe it as blood, and the Doctor confesses he could in theory even change his species. When the Doctor's amnesia passes he jigs around in happy abandon as if he has been cleansed and healed rather than haunted and wounded by his past. The only dampener is the realisation that the Master is on Earth. There is nothing bad about being a Time Lord from this Doctor's perspective. Despite this, an element of danger persists in the Doctor's reckless abandon and in his mischievous ability to remember and tell random strangers' futures. In other circumstances such lawless and thrill-seeking behaviour would be a sign of self-destructive tendencies, and his insider knowledge would be regarded as a sinister and untrustworthy power.

Although the Doctor regards the Master as 'pure evil', he chooses not to prioritise morality over science by stating matter-of-factly that 'science has shown us over and over, in the fight for survival there are no rules.' His emotions are unpredictable and hard to fathom. On the one hand he can express genuine sorrow that Puccini did not get to complete *Turandot*, but on the other it is the TARDIS who is the 'sentimental old thing' who brings Grace and Lee back from the dead. The Doctor's immediate response is not to celebrate their resurrection, but to marvel at the TARDIS and be curious about what Grace experienced in death. For a man who went to great lengths to follow the Master's dying wish in returning his remains to Gallifrey, it almost comes across as heartless when, after the Master's death, he jokes about the TARDIS' indigestion. The implication is that his original choice was governed not by compassion but by a sense of duty. Small signs though they may be, such moments point towards a darker side to the Doctor than the one he lets show.

Wild Bill Hickok

Perhaps the clearest indication that this Doctor is not as unambiguous as the Manichean good-versus-evil narrative implies is his choice of costume. Despite being popularly seen as a romantic hero, the Doctor styles himself on the frontiersman Wild Bill Hickok. In Big Finish Productions' anniversary special **Doctor Who** audio release, *The Light at the End* (2013), Nicholas Briggs makes an in-joke out of the misidentification of the outfit by having Ace call the eighth Doctor 'Byron'. Only the fourth Doctor correctly places the costume, to the delight of his future self: 'Thanks – everyone seems to think it's got something to do with Lord Byron'. But despite these historical figures coming from two very different traditions, one English, the other American, the association is not entirely misplaced.

Hickok, like Byron, amassed a cult following who idolised the character to the point of elevating him to a god-like status. His unrivalled skills with a gun were described as if they were superhero powers:

> 'The secret of Bill's success was his ability to draw and discharge his pistols, with a rapidity that was truly wonderful, and a peculiarity of his was that the two were presented and discharged simultaneously, being "out and off" before the average man had time to think about it. He never seemed to take any aim, yet he never missed.'

117

But before the desperado image had captured the public's imagination, he had been idolised as a Romantic character. Libby Custer, for instance, observed:

> 'I do not recall anything finer in the way of physical perfection than Wild Bill when he swung himself lightly from his saddle, and with graceful, swaying step, squarely set shoulders and well poised head, approached our tent for orders.'

A revisionist reading reconciles these seemingly competing versions by arguing that Wild Bill was 'gentlemanly, courteous, soft-spoken and graceful in manner,' and yet when angered would become an 'implacable enemy'[157]. Such descriptions are well suited to the eighth Doctor from his beginnings in *The Movie* to his downfall in 'The Night of the Doctor'. It is he, after all, who wilfully choses to be reborn as the War Doctor. This movement away from the Romantic hero to the desperado is reflected in the change of costume.

The association between the Doctor and Wild Bill is obscured by the fact that the legendary character, despite being prominent in popular culture, is not immediately recognisable. A revision to the script had Pete reply 'Who?' after Ted reveals who he plans to dress up as. The discarding of the gun loses much of its significance by the fact that the Doctor also dismisses a hat with equal disdain. The opportunity for the gun to remind the Doctor of his shooting is passed over because the emphasis is on the Doctor not knowing who he is. There is no obvious anti-gun message, not until he later turns a gun on himself; instead the impression given here is that the Doctor is

---

[157] Rosa, Joseph, 'Wild Bill Hickok: Pistoleer, Peace Officer and Folk Hero.'

powerful enough not to need such a primitive weapon (he has after all just shown Frankenstein-like strength in breaking out of the morgue). On one level the Doctor's anachronistic outfit reflects his naivety and lack of awareness of his surroundings post-regeneration, but on another it reflects the Doctor's rebellious stance and flamboyance, qualities that link Wild Bill and Byron.

A Tale of Two Operas

Matthew Jacobs' Doctor was partly inspired by a recent visit to see the Puccini opera, *Turandot*. The opera, based on an ancient Persian poem, recounts how Prince Calaf, while hiding his royal identity, seeks to win the hand of Princess Turandot by solving three riddles. Having succeeded in his quest, when Turandot makes it clear to her father that she wants to be released from the commitment to marry the stranger, Calaf sets her a riddle of his own to give her a chance to win back her freedom. Turandot's challenge is to tell Calaf his name within 24 hours. Desperate not to marry him, she threatens to kill the entire population of the city unless the name is uncovered. In the process Calaf loses the one person who truly loved him, his family's slave Liu, who dies refusing to reveal Calaf's name. Impressed by Lui's resoluteness, Turandot asks how she can keep silent, to which Liu replies 'Love'. At the end of the opera Turandot, having been instantly wooed by Calaf's kiss, declares 'His name is love'[158].

'His name is love' was central to the original plot of Jacob's script. When Grace is bleeped while at the opera, Turandot would have been about to guess the name of her suitor. At this stage in Jacob's

---

[158] For full transcripts and translations of the librettos of *Turandot* and *Madam Butterfly* see 'DM's Opera Site'.

thinking the Doctor's name plays a crucial role in the revealing of his identity. When masquerading as a medical Doctor he even calls himself 'Dr Who'[159]. Grace's kiss with the Doctor is similarly transformative, instantly turning the sceptical surgeon into a lovestruck puppy. Subsequent drafts gave even more significance to *Turandot*. 'His name is love' are words that Grace speaks over the seventh Doctor on the operating table, and the eighth Doctor confirms his identity by later repeating them. The symbolism of the opera is heightened still further by the Doctor encountering his childhood self in the Eye of Harmony, immediately after his mother saves his life. The child Doctor asks who the stranger is, to which the eighth Doctor replies, 'My name is love'[160]

Casting aside the central play on Calaf's mysterious identity, the character shares little kinship with the Doctor. Calaf callously disregards the safety of his father and the love of his slave-girl Liu in his single-minded drive to gain Turandot's hand in marriage. Even after Liu has sacrificed her life to protect his secret, Calaf continues to pursue Turandot despite calling her the Princess of Death. It is clear that, in the original draft of *The Movie*, 'his name is love' is stripped of all irony as the Doctor is modelled as a godlike figure[161]. For him the name is entirely appropriate. The analogies between Grace and Turandot are also only skin deep. Apart from becoming equally besotted after a kiss, and trying to solve the mystery of a stranger's identity, they share nothing in common.

Due to the excessive cost of using the aria from *Turandot*, a decision

---

[159] Segal with Russell, *Regeneration*, p102.
[160] *The Complete History* #47, p68.
[161] Compare *I John* 4.8, 'God is love.'

was made to switch to the cheaper *Madam Butterfly*, with some of the producers believing that little would be lost since the subtle references would have gone over most viewers' heads[162]. Nevertheless, traces of Jacobs' original vision remain in the movie, not least the explicit foreshadowing in the stock music used for the seventh Doctor's opening scene. 'In a Dream (I Called out your Name)' highlights the centrality of the search for the Doctor's identity and the prominent role of the kiss:

> 'I called out your name
> in a misty dream last night.
> Saw that old smile that I miss.
> It was a beautiful sight.
> Your kiss was a flame,
> not the spark that somehow died,
> and every warm embrace
> was real as all those tears I've cried.'

The fact that Puccini died before he could finish *Turandot* is mentioned by the Doctor, in what could be interpreted as a meta-reference to the open-ended nature of the end of the series' original run. Though tempting, such a reading must surely be accidentally ironic rather than intended by the author, given that Alfano's work in completing the opera is seen at best as a serviceable solution to an almost insurmountable hole that Puccini had allegedly written himself into, with one critic calling it 'hack work'[163].

Disproving the producers' point about fandom, in August 1996 a

---

162 See Appendix 2.
163 Clements, Andrew, 'I Think it's all Over'.

speculative article appeared in a New Zealand fanzine arguing the case for Grace being the Doctor's mother[164]. The repeated references to *Madam Butterfly* are cited as evidence in support of this elaborate theory. The writer, Neil Lambess, notes that the Doctor, like Sorrow (or 'Trouble' in the English short story the opera was adapted from), the son of Madam Butterfly and Pilkington, is a child born of two very different cultures, who loses his human mother to be raised by his father. In such a reading, Japan stands for Earth and America for Gallifrey. The article is a marvellous example of the art of fan speculation, or as the Doctor would put it, 'humans [...] seeing patterns in things that aren't there.'

The quote has been all too often used as a discussion breaker, or a putdown in various **Doctor Who** online forums, but the eighth Doctor celebrates this essential feature of the human mind, prefacing the observation with 'I love humans.' Making links, and finding meaning out of seemingly disconnected events and occurrences, are how worldviews are constructed.

Lambess' speculative association between the Doctor and Sorrow is stitched into a larger pattern in order to identify Grace as the Doctor's mother. In his novelisation, Gary Russell goes to the opposite extreme but nonetheless still finds a connection: 'Appropriately enough, the lullaby Butterfly sings to her baby son Sorrow, "Dormi Amor Mio", began as Grace stared as her comatose patient.'[165] Appropriate, presumably, only because the Doctor, like

---

[164] Lambess, Neil, 'A State of Temporal Grace', *Time/Space Visualiser* #46, August 1997.
[165] Russell, *The Novel of the Film*, p40. If there was any intentional link between Grace and the Doctor's mother, then surely the final

Sorrow, is not awake.

Instead of identifying the Doctor with Sorrow, there are other possible symbolic connections that, although unintended by the writer, have more mileage before they collapse into the fanciful. In sharp contrast to the resonance of 'His Name is Love', lyrically the aria 'Un Bel Di' makes no sense as an implicit commentary of the plot of *The Movie*. Three years after Pilkington leaves Japan to return to the USA, Madam Butterfly (Cio Cio) expresses her blind faith in her American husband, believing that he will return to her. In 'Un Bel Di' she imagines his ship arriving in the port, depicting herself not as a submissive wife but as one who controls how their reconciliation will take place, teasing him by not going to meet him. This self-image is consistently undermined in the opera by a Western exotic view of Japanese women.

Puccini's orientalism is in marked contrast to the presentation of San Francisco's Chinese community in *The Movie*, and Grace shares none of Cio Cio's naivety, but the clash of cultures and the relationship between identity and nationality are themes that connect the two. Like Pilkington, the Doctor can feel passionately for Grace, but ultimately cannot fully embrace her culture or her people. The two

---

aria, 'Tu Tu Piccolo Iddio', would have been selected for this scene:
> 'Look well, well
> on your mother's face,
> that you may keep a faint memory of it,
> look well!
> Little love, farewell!
> Farewell, my little love!
> Go and play.'

characters can be both intimate and detached.

Cio Cio can also be likened to Grace in that both characters are caught between two worlds. Cio Cio alienates herself from her people as she converts to Western religion and culture, yet she can only express her love through traditional Japanese music. The repeated use of the Star Spangled Banner theme feels at best like an unnatural interruption and at worst like the sinister beats of Western imperialism. Madam Butterfly ends in tragedy with Cio Cio's suicide, and although Grace's story has an upbeat conclusion, with the promise of greater things to come – at least according to the Doctor's mysterious predictions – her life has been turned upside-down and it is not clear how she will be able to recover.

THE DOCTOR'S NEMESIS

The decision to feature the Master in *The Movie* was largely a question of expediency. With instructions not to include the Daleks, Matthew Jacobs very quickly settled on the malevolent Time Lord as the main antagonist[166]. An opponent with a human appearance provided an opportunity to cast a big-name American star, thus fulfilling the producer's obligations to Fox. With the BBC insistent on a British actor to play the Doctor, and with the inherent difficulties in attracting a star to take on a regular companion role despite only being contracted for a single movie, writing a one-off, scene-stealing villain for an American actor was the most logical way forward. As the Master, not only would the actor draw in an audience for *The Movie*, he would also be inducted into **Doctor Who** canon as the latest incarnation of one of the show's most iconic characters.

The Master was also an ideal fit for Jacobs' 'Who am I?' narrative, in that he embodies the alien aspect of the Doctor and functions as an essential link to his Gallifreyan origins. He is first and foremost the Doctor's nemesis, with the Earth little more than an accidental playing field upon which he can realise his ambitions, but equally important is the fact that he is the Doctor's compatriot.

Literary villains come in all shapes and sizes and have been classified in a variety of ways. The Master in *The Movie* embodies the traits of several archetypical antagonists. The requirements of the story itself, the history of the character, Eric Roberts' delivery and interpretation,

---

[166] See Appendix 2. The Master, despite featuring in both the Leekley and DeLaurentis scripts, was not one of the elements that Segal included in his brief to Jacobs.

and the wider aims of the production all contributed different aspects that, whilst not always compatible, ultimately came together to create one of the show's most memorable villains.

The Antithesis of the Doctor

Throughout the adventure the two characters are set up as polar opposites, so much so that it is no exaggeration to describe the Master as 'Who am I not?' from the Doctor's perspective[167]. Both characters have cheated death – the Doctor through regeneration and the Master through assuming a morphant form that is able to possess a body of his choosing. Just as the Doctor has Grace, the Master has a companion in Chang Lee. Both characters position themselves outside the human race as godlike observers and commentators, and yet are unable to separate themselves from the human. Whilst the Doctor enthusiastically embraces his human side, the Master is hell bent on freeing himself from the limitations of his human body. Both find significance in their choice of clothing, with the Doctor casually donning the costume of a maverick freedom fighter and the Master the regal robes of a Time Lord with high office.

If the characters' costumes symbolise their opposition, then so too does their use, non-use and misuse of accessories. The Doctor rejects guns, whilst the Master weaponises Time Lord artefacts[168]. The Doctor brings poverty in his wake, with Grace losing her career and partner, whereas the Master promises vast wealth to Chang

---

[167] Note how the Doctor's primal 'Who am I?' is intercut with shots of the Master reborn with Bruce's face.

[168] In the novelisation Russell describes him as using the sceptre of Rassilon as a fighting staff (Russell, *The Novel of the Film*, p212).

Lee[169]. The Doctor is unable to make Grace any promises of future bliss or protection from death ('I can't make your dream come true forever Grace, but I can make it come true today'), whilst the Master tempts Chang Lee with inexhaustible wealth and happiness. The Doctor takes the driver's seat on the motorbike, whereas Chang Lee drives the ambulance under the Master's instructions. Even their mannerisms are contrasted, with the Doctor dancing in the shoes that fit and the Master walking stiltedly, clearly uncomfortable in his new skin. The Doctor discards the past in order to embrace his new life (rejecting the familiar scarf), whereas the Master is bitterly driven by what he has lost and sets about trying to undo the past.

The Embodiment of Evil

The Doctor once warned the Sea Devils not to trust the Master, calling him 'the personification of evil'[170]. It is the least subtle use of the villain, in that for evil to be set free from any shades of grey there can be no psychological or biographical reasons for its existence. Evil is at its darkest when stripped of motivation or explanation. Evil for evil's sake has sometimes been the forte of the Master, but there is little evidence of this approach in *The Movie*, despite the fact that

---

[169] Although *The Movie* finishes with the Doctor giving Chang Lee the gold dust, there is no grand gesture involved, certainly nothing like the kind we see in more recent **Doctor Who**, such as the Doctor's Santa act in *The Doctor, the Widow and the Wardrobe* (2011), or Rory's car and Amy and Rory's house in *The God Complex* (2011) with its TARDIS blue door reminding his friends of the source of their wealth. Instead, it is almost like an afterthought. It might even be that very human thing of getting the proverbial gooseberry out of the way.

[170] *The Sea Devils* episode 5 (1972).

Jacobs uses that expression in his original pitch, and the Doctor tells Grace he is 'pure evil'.

Not only are all the Master's actions necessary to his ambitions, there is no sign here that he is revelling in the suffering of others. Bruce's wife and the security guards are dispatched with efficiency, the former is followed by only the slightest of unscripted smiles and the latter occurs off screen. This version of the Master takes more delight in his own importance and in his ability to manipulate others with words than he does in exacting violence.

On the other hand, the Master lacks any sympathetic treatment. He is introduced as a criminal whose life has been forfeited because of his heinous crimes. There is no exploration as to why those crimes were committed in the first place. There is a logic to his efforts to steal the Doctor's regenerations, but despite the Byronic roots of its hero, the movie steers away from the Romantic notion that the fallen angel might also have reason to feel aggrieved. Without the luxury of a full season of stories to build worlds and develop rounded characters, inevitably some had to be stripped of layers of complexity and play a functional role by inhabiting certain stereotypes.

The Master embodies evil only insofar as there was insufficient time to explore his character in any depth. By way of justification for the one-dimensional nature of the character, until the final scenes he is characterised as unaffected. Any display of emotion is an act, and a pretty poor one at that. Even the Daleks noticed his unnatural 'calmness' as he faced execution, and when Chang Lee is no longer required, the 'son he never had' is killed with emotionless efficiency. The realisation that the Doctor has scuppered his plans again finally provokes his first act in anger, as the feral side of the degenerate

Master comes out in full force.

The Doctor's Moriarty

The Master was born out of the need to add variety to the Doctor's earthbound stories in the 1970s. Barry Letts and Terrance Dicks, conscious of the Sherlock Holmes and Dr Watson dynamic between the third Doctor and the Brigadier, decided to introduce a Moriarty figure as a recurring character[171]. The Master's uniqueness as an enemy stems from the fact that he is the Doctor's equal in intellect and will. As with Holmes and Moriarty, the pair share a mutual appreciation. The name 'Master' highlights this intentional symmetry: both renegades have adopted a pseudonym from the world of academia.

The novelist Anthony Horowitz has identified five reasons why Moriarty could be viewed as the definitive nemesis character[172]:

An Association With Death

Moriarty is one of several well-known villains whose names are etymologically related to death (e.g. Darth Vader, Mordred and Voldemort). Death is the one enemy that no individual can defeat. In *The Movie* the Master is attempting the impossible, continuing an obsession first introduced in *The Deadly Assassin* and which later characterised Anthony Ainley's performance. In Jacobs' earlier synopses the theme is made more explicit with the Halloween setting, and the revivification of Chang Lee's father and others. The association of the Master with death would go on to be used to great

---

[171] Letts, Barry, *Who & Me*, p125.
[172] Horowitz, Anthony, 'Sherlock v Moriarty: Perfect Foes'.

effect in the revived series, with the Master reborn (*The End of Time* (2009-10)), Missy's army of the resurrected which adds a Cyber-twist and a new motivation to Jacobs' original idea (*Dark Water / Death in Heaven* (2014)), Missy's 'execution' (*Extremis* (2017)) and the two Masters at the heart of a new Cybermen origin story (*World Enough and Time / The Doctor Falls* (2017)).

A Gentleman Who Has Never Killed Anyone

The veil of respectability that keeps Moriarty above suspicion is a constant source of frustration for Holmes, making him a formidable opponent. Always covering his tracks and relying on henchmen to do his dirty work, Moriarty is safely distanced from his crimes. Villains who are gratuitously violent or grotesque in their behaviour are less sinister than these wolves in sheep's clothing and far less dangerous. Whilst the Master could never be accused of keeping his hands clean (he commits murder in his first story, *Terror of the Autons* (1971)), charm offensives and cloak-and-dagger approaches are typical. In many of his earliest outings the Master ingratiates himself into positions of authority, albeit often relying on hypnotic suggestion or disguises. He manipulates behind the scenes, hiding behind a more immediate threat (Autons, Axons, Sea Devils, etc.) and more often than not uses henchmen (e.g. Ogrons) to do his dirty work.

But whilst he does have Chang Lee at his beck and call, in *The Movie* the Master's methods are unsubtle and his crimes barely disguised. In that respect the desperate nature of his current plight makes him more of a precursor to the Master reborn in *The End of Time*, than John Simm's original Harold Saxon guise. Horowitz argues that the 'less is more' principle is one worth noting when writing archenemies, pointing out that Hannibal Lecter is a far more chilling character in the first two books in the series (*Red Dragon* (1981) and *The Silence of the Lambs* (1988)), in which he is less centre-stage. At one point, fearing that he had gone overboard with the Master's theatrical speeches, Jacobs made numerous cuts, only to end up putting most of them back in. Eric Roberts was particularly enamoured of the scenes in question and had already memorised his lines[173].

The Master in all his guises does have a tendency to playfully send himself up with the over-the-top archness of a Bond villain. Naming himself 'the Master' should be enough of a clue that this has always been a feature of his temperament. Even the suave and cool Roger Delgado incarnation embraces the theatre of the megalomaniac, most notably when attiring himself in ecclesiastical robes in *The Dæmons* (1971).

Literate and Well-Spoken

From Moriarty to Dr No, the incongruent juxtaposition of evil intent with a politeness of speech is a hallmark of some of the most memorable villains. By contrast, regional accents tend to be the preserve of the 'lovable rogue' trope. There is something paradoxically British about Eric Roberts' version of the Master, particularly when (in an unscripted ad lib) he corrects Grace's grammar, but perhaps more generally based on the often-used American convention of casting a British actor as the antagonist. Like the Doctor's transformation of the gunslinger Bill Hickok costume into that of the Byronic gentleman, the Master, despite being played by an American, transcends the trappings of the culture he has

---

[173] See Appendix 2.

assumed[174]. There is little hint of the working man Bruce, with the Master channelling instead his English precursors. Roberts' American accent is one of the reasons why such an interpretation appears to be pantomimic. There is a certain artificial quality to the performance that gives the false impression that the actor is sending up the show. Imagine the very same scenes played by either Delgado or Ainley and simply by virtue of their accent they would come across as more natural and therefore less camp.

A Striking Appearance

> 'He is extremely tall and thin, his forehead domes out in a white curve, and his two eyes are deeply sunken in his head. He is clean-shaven, pale, and ascetic-looking, retaining something of the professor in his features. His shoulders are rounded from much study, and his face protrudes forward, and is for ever slowly oscillating from side to side in a curiously reptilian fashion.'
>
> [Arthur Conan Doyle, 'The Final Problem']

Memorable uber-villains are often set apart by their outlandish appearance or by some unusual physical feature or deformity. From Moriarty to the motley line-up of Batman villains, the archenemy catches the eye, drawing attention to themselves as objects of attraction or fear.

The Master's appearance in *The Movie* was originally intended to be grotesque, with Bruce's body rapidly degenerating (thus making more sense of the Master's urgency in finding a new body), but the

---

[174] Roger Delgado's original Master also came across as unspecifically 'foreign'.

results proved to be impractical and uncomfortable for the actor. Instead the Master's possession of Bruce was conveyed through the green snake-eyes contact lenses, giving him a reptilian quality in keeping with the Moriarty analogy. Even these, however, irritated Roberts so as a further compromise the dark sunglasses were introduced. Roberts was also unhappy with the original costume. A black futuristic version of the Roger Delgado suit had been designed to contrast with the Doctor's period garb, but at the actor's behest it was replaced with the long leather jacket. As a compromise the plan was to save the Cardin-Nehru design for the final TARDIS scenes, but it clashed with the darkness of the cloister room (hence the use of traditional Time Lord robes). Nevertheless, despite the Master now blending in with the crowd far more effectively than the Doctor, signs of the abnormal remain, such as when he picks off his fingernails, and those moments when his gait is stilted or his speech unnaturally intoned.

He Must Always Expect to be Beaten by His Nemesis

Like Moriarty and Holmes the Master and the Doctor hold each other in high regard, but neither pair have formed a mutual admiration society. Moriarty and the Master are obsessed with winning, a compulsion born of an implicit fear of failure. Whilst blessed with exceptional intelligence and learning, they are primarily driven by a childish schoolboy rivalry and the will to get one over on their rival. As Alan Barnes notes, the Master's very first scheme is 'nothing more than a variant of the old "bucket of water over teacher" trick practiced by fictional fourth-formers the galaxy over.'[175] This rivalry

---

[175] Barnes, Alan, 'The Duelling Master', *The Essential Doctor Who* #4: *The Master*, cover date March 2015, p33.

is effectively parodied in Steven Moffat's comic relief sketch, *The Curse of Fatal Death*, with Jonathan Pryce camping it up as a Master who never knows when he is beaten.

The eighth Doctor describes the Master as 'a rival Time Lord', but any admiration from the Doctor's side is entirely absent from the script. In the version of the script released by BBC Books, in a marked departure from the norm the Doctor does not even try to save his old friend at the end, and in the story as broadcast there is no attempt to reason with him or turn him towards a less drastic course[176]. Jacobs' interest is not so much in the Master and the Doctor's backstories but in the mythological possibilities of their ancient rivalry, calling it a 'primal conflict'[177].

The Devil in Disguise

In much the same way as John Leekley had taken inspiration from Greek mythology, Matthew Jacobs' original ideas were rooted in Judaeo-Christian religion. The Doctor was not originally likened to Christ[178], but the Master was written with Jesus' rival, Satan, very firmly in mind:

- He literally takes the form of a serpent.
- He possesses human beings.

---

[176] *Planet of Fire* (1984) is the one time when the Doctor walks away with the Master begging him to save him, but usually when given the opportunity the Doctor reaches out to the Master, who in turn usually refuses his offer of salvation (*Survival, Last of the Time Lords*), not wanting to be obligated to him or to be on the road to reform.
[177] Segal with Russell, *Regeneration*, p101.
[178] He is not even likened to a prophet; instead he is simply 'a great man' (Segal with Russell, *Regeneration*, p101).

- He is a tempter and manipulator.
- He desires to be the god of the universe.
- He is seeking to recover that which was lost.
- He presents himself as the hero.
- He wants to turn the Earth into a literal hell.
- He is a destructive and corrupting force.

Whilst Jacobs was determined not to get bogged down in continuity concerns, with the exception of the Master's morphant snake form (though c.f. his transmogrification into a Cheetah Person in *Survival*) all of the above had been aspects of the archvillain and his evil schemes during the 70s and 80s. He possesses the body of Nyssa's father Tremas (*The Keeper of Traken* (1980)), he promises Goth the presidency of Gallifrey (*The Deadly Assassin*), he explicitly states his desire to become a god (*Colony in Space* (1971)), he is variously searching for freedom, immortality and a new body or lifecycle, he pretends to be working in the Earth's interests whether as a politician, military man, vicar or scientist, and on numerous occasions he attempts to start a devastating war involving Earth.

Not all of these elements made it to the final script[179], but there were enough to in turn push the characterisation of the Doctor away from the anti-hero that Segal had been looking for. Inevitably, with a longstanding and unreconstructed Satan-like rival set up as his polar opposite, the Doctor is forced into playing the role of the archetypical force for good. The Christ-like allusions become unavoidable.

The modelling of the character on a pre-Milton monstrous Satan not

---

[179] The quest for godhood and immortality is replaced by the quest for the Doctor's remaining lives and the Earth is no longer of any interest.

only deifies the hero, it also adds a certain campness to the villain. We have already seen that there are no efforts here to make the Master an anti-villain, or to turn convention on its head by presenting the villain as wronged or admirable, leaving Roberts to conclude:

> 'He's a real melodramatic over-the-top evil character. So it's like playing the bad guy when you're eight years old and you have the biggest gun. It's not really like you're getting into evilness. You're getting into Halloween.'[180]

The notion of the devil in disguise offers the possibility of a more nuanced take on the good-versus-evil conflict, one that is freed from the limitations of a dualistic worldview that for centuries had been misapplied to the original literary figures from the Old Testament. As Percy Shelley concludes of the devil in Milton's *Paradise Lost*:

> 'Nothing can exceed the energy and magnificence of the character of Satan as expressed in *Paradise Lost*. It is a mistake to suppose that he could ever have been intended for the popular personification of evil.'[181]

The Romantic reading of Milton, best exemplified by Blake's assessment that he was 'a true Poet [...] of the Devils party without knowing it,'[182] is however a distorted picture. Milton is as much governed by his religious beliefs as he is by the poetic imagination. The egotistical Satan, whilst given a human face and presented as

---

[180] Quoted in Rigby, Jonathan, 'The Trick or Treat Master', *The Essential Doctor Who: The Master*, p97.
[181] Shelley, Percy Bysshe, *A Defence of Poetry*, 1821, in *Selected Poems and Prose*, 2017.
[182] Blake, William, *The Marriage of Heaven and Hell*, circa 1790-1793.

eminently more relatable than the monstrous and horned version, is ultimately thwarted in his quest for power.

Paradise Lost shows that it is possible to write a character who can be irredeemably evil whilst at the same time having qualities that could be considered admirable. As Chris Culver observes, such villains are generally the most fascinating:

> 'a good villain is one who's exceptional for something in addition to his villainy. He's witty, he's charming, he's, quite possibly, the most interesting man in the world. A good villain isn't just a regular person who does bad things.'[183]

The Pantomime Villain

In 1996 Matthew Jacobs correctly predicted that the characterisation of the Master in *The Movie* would become a major talking point: '**Doctor Who** fans will be very interested to look at how the Master is portrayed.'[184] Eric Roberts' performance continues to be one of the most talked-about aspects of the movie, with many believing that the character was ill-judged[185]. The campness of the performance for some verges on the parodic – a sending-up of the show (on a par with *The Curse of Fatal Death*'s Master) and a disservice to the previous actors to have played the role.

When Steven Moffat was asked if he had considered bringing Eric Roberts back for the multi-Master series 10 finale, he admitted that it hadn't even crossed his mind:

---

[183] Culver, Chris, 'What Makes a Good Villain?'
[184] Gillatt, 'Urban Regeneration', p13.
[185] See Appendix 1.

'I like that TV movie and I liked him as the Master, I thought he was funny. But he's not part […] of anyone's pantheon of **Doctor Who**. Not because he didn't do well – he did do it well – and not because that film isn't good – it is quite good – it's just not really there. John Simm absolutely had a presence in the audience's mind as the Master and that counted. Just as Roger Delgado and Anthony Ainley still have a presence in people's minds as the Master. But it has to be, iconically, the Master versus, iconically, the Master.'[186]

It's a rather peculiar explanation given than Moffat had already effectively made *The Movie* part of the established canon in 'The Night of the Doctor'. It is tempting to suggest that not being 'really there' is another way of saying it was 'way out there'. Too camp, too over-the-top even for the 21st-century series. There are far less controversial and indeed easier ways of explaining why Roberts wasn't considered – a rights issue fudge, the fact that Bruce's body will have been completely decayed even if he did survive the Eye of Harmony, or simply that it did not suit the story[187].

The BBC and those involved in *The Movie*'s production are understandably far less dismissive than Moffat. However, rather than embracing the camp, something that writer Matthew Jacobs has no qualms about, most of the key players have been presenting a counternarrative that started during post-production.

Eric Roberts insisted that he would only accept the role following

[186] McEwan, Cameron, 'Steven Moffat Reveals Why He Didn't Bring Eric Roberts Back to **Doctor Who** as the Master'.
[187] Although notably the character reappears in short stories and a forthcoming audio drama from Big Finish.

assurances that he could play the character straight: 'I want to scare the crap out of people. What can we say to get you do it? Let me play it real. They said go, you can do it – with runny nose and glassy eyes.'[188] The BBC for their part were nervous of anything that might be reflective of the camper and cornier tones of the series during John Nathan-Turner's tenure.

In an interview conducted shortly before *The Movie* aired, Geoffrey Sax was at pains to highlight the realism behind Eric Roberts' characterisation of the Master: 'The thing about Eric is that he can be very frightening, but he still keeps it within the framework of **Doctor Who**. He's not camp or anything like that, he's genuinely scary.'[189]

The anti-camp narrative has continued long after the 1996 broadcast. Roberts recalls that when asked by his agent if he was interested in the role, he replied:

> 'I want to play him real. I don't want to play him campy! ... say "Eric knows how you want him played campy, but Eric doesn't want to play that." He came back and said they were fine with it...'[190]

All of the above smacks of protesting too much, and unnecessarily so. There is an inherent parodic element to the character of the Master that lends itself to the camp. Lance Parkin calls him the 'ultimate rent-a-villain', arguing that unlike the Daleks he can be

---

[188] Interviewed in Tilley, Doug, and Liam O'Donnell, 'The Eric Roberts is the Fucking Man Podcast', episode 62.
[189] Gillatt, Gary, 'Renaissance'. DWM #238, p13.
[190] Quoted in Matt Adams, 'The Best Dressed', DWM #497.

shoehorned into any story[191]. As a stand-in or shorthand for evil he is the most generic of villains. If there are any motivations behind his evil schemes then they are one-dimensional and uncomplicated. *The Movie* is the most blatant expression of how the Master has always been written.

Jacobs is well aware of the oversimplification of the Master in *The Movie*, arguing that he lacked the opportunity to explore the character in any depth because of the constraints of the one-off movie format. He also puts the campness of the performance down to Eric Roberts' interpretation and the actor's fondness for British pantomime[192], a curious suggestion given Roberts' negative views of the campness of **Doctor Who**.

The theatricality and the more comedic elements of the Master in *The Movie* have a number of roots. On the one hand they are an essential aspect of the character and an inescapable consequence of writing him as the archetypal villain, and on the other they are down to Eric Roberts' delivery. The efforts to create a distinctive feel for the show, and to set it apart from other series, also impacted on the way the character was written and performed.

The Leekley script, which had already featured the Master heavily, was deemed to have been far too convoluted and confusing. It was further criticised for lacking the wit, charm and humour of the original show. Robert DeLaurentis, tasked with writing an alternative script, proposed a major tonal shift:

---

[191] Parkin, Lance, 'The Galaxy's Most Wanted', DWM #311, cover date December 2001, p9.
[192] See Appendix 2.

'it takes itself too seriously. Not only should it be funnier, but more "fun" that is, more of a romp, a wild weekly rollercoaster ride. Right now it's dark and inaccessible, weighed down with unnecessary science fiction baggage. It needs to be a bright, human adventure.'[193]

In order to set apart **Doctor Who** from other science fiction shows such as **The X-Files** and **Babylon 5**, the Master is written as a straight up, in your face bad guy, in contrast to the shadowy Cigarette-Smoking Man[194], and the Vorlons and Shadows with their competing philosophies.

Camp in this context should then be seen as a positive quality, even though in was a tone the BBC were too embarrassed to own publicly. It is also a largely unintended and unavoidable aspect of a show that has never taken itself too seriously:

'**Doctor Who**'s highly developed sense of warm self-parody, along with the series' habit of presenting life-or-death issues against a backdrop of playfulness and whimsy, makes it particularly prone to unintentional campery.'[195]

The Disturbed Personality

Popular fictional villains (and indeed heroes) often fall somewhere within the 'Dark Triad' of Machiavellianism, narcissism and

---

[193] Segal with Russell, *Regeneration*, p70.
[194] The conspiracy angle popularised by **The X-Files** is initially set up in the guise of Swift burning the x-rays of the alien Doctor, but is placed there as a red herring.
[195] Gillatt, Gary, *Doctor Who from A to Z* (1998), p61.

psychopathy[196]. Such characters, both in real life and in film and TV, tend to be well-groomed and physically attractive, a feature certainly true of the Delgado, Ainley, Simm and Gomez incarnations. The degenerate version as seen in *The Deadly Assassin* and *The Keeper of Traken* is totally consumed by hate, having lost his ability to deceive and be admired. Vanity is one of several weaknesses the Doctor is able to exploit (*Terror of the Autons*). Whilst the insanity of the Master is particularly emphasised in the 21st-century series[197], with John Simm describing him as 'the ultimate narcissist (who) fancies himself,'[198] the character has regularly displayed all three points of the triad.

The Narcissist

Narcissism's unique contribution to the Dark Triad is the sense of entitlement and superiority. Contemporary psychologists have

---

[196] Jonason, Peter, Gregory Webster, David Schmitt, Norman Lii and Laura Crysel, 'The Antihero in Popular Culture: A Life History Theory of the Dark Triad,' *Review of General Psychology* 16(2), 2012, p192. The term was first introduced by Paulus, Delroy and Kevin Williams in their influential paper 'The Dark Triad of Personality: Narcissism, Machiavellianism, and Psychopathy,' *Journal of Research in Personality* 36, 2002.

[197] Russell T Davies actively avoided using the term 'evil' (quoted in Martin, 'Who Do We Think We Are?'):

> 'The moment you say someone is evil, you've stopped any understanding of them or any chance of helping them, or any chance of reducing their numbers. It's a really wrong thing to do. Other writers will put the word "evil" in, and I absolutely tell them to take it out.'

[198] Quoted in Cook, Benjamin, 'New Life for the Old Master', DWM #514, p25.

identified different types of narcissistic personalities, including vulnerable narcissism in which individuals base their self-image on the approval of others, and grandiose narcissism in which individuals flaunt their self-assessed qualities. One helpful way of distinguishing between the two would be to imagine both saying 'Look at me.' The vulnerable narcissist emphasises 'look' and the grandiose narcissist emphasises 'me'. Both are self-absorbed and lack empathy, but one acts through low self-esteem and the other through a deluded sense of their own brilliance.

Prior to *The Movie* the Master had displayed both types, with his degenerate form bringing an unwelcome vulnerability and an emotionally-driven quest for revenge that is a stark departure from the suave and cold Delgado incarnation. Delgado's grandiose narcissism is well evidenced in *The Dæmons*: 'to do my will shall be the whole of the law!' Back in a new body, a vain mirror of his pre-Tersurus appearance, the Ainley Master's narcissism is even more marked and is firmly back to its original grandiose state. He even starts to wear disguises for his own amusement, or because the world itself is treated as his captive audience (*Time-Flight* (1982)).

The Movie's Master is an odd fusion of the original Delgado version and the degenerate Master from *The Deadly Assassin*, because although he has cheated death by taking possession of another body, unlike the Ainley Master, the crisis is far from over. The perilous nature of his predicament would have been clearer had his decaying appearance been retained from the original script. He is neither one thing nor another and without time on his side, his grandiose 'I always dress for the occasion' personality is a cover-up for a more vulnerable dying figure, desperate to be brought to new life. Jacobs pays tribute to Delgado's incarnation, but his strongest memories of

Doctor Who were of Hartnell, Troughton and Tom Baker's eras. It is not surprising then that his Master is not primarily based on the original. The Eye of Harmony, the Rassilon references, the framing of the Doctor as the villain, the Time Lord outfit, and the Master's desperate quest for survival instead all call to mind Robert Holmes' *The Deadly Assassin*. Jacobs' first outlines share an even stronger affinity with the 1976 myth-building serial, with the Master's body becoming completely monstrous and with the final showdown between the two Time Lords taking place in an alternative reality[199].

The Psychopath

David Layton argues that **Doctor Who** villains are rarely psychopathic because harming people is not their primary goal. He prefers to describe them as psychologically damaged. They are all reacting in extreme ways to an existential sense of alienation, by either taking mastery over the world or by submitting to a controlling power. For Layton, the Master is an example of the former and the hive-minded Daleks the latter. The insanity comes from ironically losing contact with the world in this process, with the Master for instance seeing his environment as a reflection of himself[200].

Certainly, if we were to look at some of the most iconic movie psychopaths there are no clear equivalents in **Doctor Who**, but in order to rule out psychopathy as a quality of the Master we would have to resist assessing the character merely according to distorted

---

[199] Segal with Russell, *Regeneration,* p102. Initially Jacobs describes it as a 'truly sci-fi setting.' In the more detailed second outline the Eye of Harmony is the entrance into a mirror reality, a surreal twist on this universe which frightens the Master because of its beauty.
[200] Layton, David, *The Humanism of Doctor Who*, p192.

screen stereotypes. More accurate benchmarks can be found in the clinical literature about the complex. Layton can only really distinguish psychopathy from insanity by narrowly reading the condition as a trope of fiction.

Early movie psychopaths tended to be socially rejected misfits driven by revenge. They were largely the preserve of the slash horror genre[201]. As such they were obviously fictional figures, creatures from the surreal realm of our nightmares. During the 1990s psychopaths, many of them supposedly based on real-world equivalents, appeared as major characters in at least 51 movies, more so than any other decade to date[202]. The old school arch characters were less prevalent in this era, with the focus now, at least in intention, on realistic horror and crime. Antony Hopkins' Hannibal Lecter (*The Silence of the Lambs* (1991)) quickly became the archetypical psychopath as far as the entertainment industry was concerned, despite being regarded by psychologists as one of the least realistic psychopathic characters[203]. The industry has now moved on somewhat, with more nuanced and believable screen psychopaths (e.g. *No Country for Old Men* (2007)), but the character still holds sway over the popular imagination[204].

---

[201] Examples include Norman Bates (*Psycho* (1960)), Michael Myers (*Halloween* (1978) and sequels)) and Jason Vorhees (*Friday the 13th* (1980) and sequels) (Swart, Joan, 'Psychopaths in Films', in Arntfield, Michael, and Marcel Danesi, eds, *The Critical Humanities: An Introduction*, p82).

[202] Swart, 'Psychopaths in Films', p84.

[203] See Leistedt, Samuel, and Paul Linkowski 'Psychopathy and the Cinema: Fact or Fiction?' *Journal of Forensic Sciences* #59, 2014.

[204] Swart, 'Psychopaths in Films', pp85-86.

The Master in *The Movie* falls somewhere between the monstrous and predatory misfits of the 1960s to 80s and the calculating and sophisticated genius of Hannibal Lecter. Both character types are exaggerated, twisted versions of psychopaths who would ironically fail to be recognised as such by clinicians. Diagnosing the Master is much easier, and of the various subtypes of psychopaths one in particular resonates:

> 'The covetous psychopath displays envy and revenge as core characteristics. They are exhibitionistic and self-indulgent as they relentlessly pursue aggrandizement, believing that they have been deprived of their rightful share of love, support, and material rewards. In the process they often have little concern for the people that they deceive and exploit.'[205]

The Machiavellian

'Whereas narcissism describes an excessive self-aggrandisement and psychopathy involves an antisocial nature lacking in empathic concern, Machiavellianism is characterized by a manipulative, self-serving social strategy with three main components: cynicism, manipulativeness, and a view that the ends justify the means.'[206]

'High Machs' are hugely competitive, driven by a need to win. To that end other people become pawns in their game, ready to be sacrificed at the opportune time. They are exploitative, persuasive, and masters of deception. Their ruthlessness is unashamed and their lack of morals often self-proclaimed. They thrive in unstructured, unsupervised work environments.

---

[205] Swart, 'Psychopaths in Films', p80.
[206] Jonason et al, 'The Antihero in Popular Culture', p195.

Most psychopaths lack self-awareness, but the Master knows exactly what he is doing and why. This is the Machiavellian point of the triad at work. The Master is hardly psychologically ignorant (as he demonstrates to Grace in the discussion over transference). The high Mach in him also adds that deliberate, premediated quality to his schemes which might otherwise be chaotic and poorly thought through[207]. Of itself, Machiavellianism is not especially self-aggrandising, but when combined with the narcissist's sense of entitlement and the psychopath's fixation on causing harm we are presented with the kind of personality that characterises the Eric Roberts Master. Behind the camp façade and good-versus-evil narrative is indeed a more complex character: a master orator whose specialist subject is himself, a villain in touch with and rather proud of his own evilness, and a prima donna driven by a desire to be adored. How good he is at the Machiavellian point of the triad is another matter entirely, but the bypassing of the usual channels of persuasion with hypnosis, while reflecting the urgency of his situation, is entirely consistent with his first incarnation who, though more than able to play the long game (*The Mind of Evil* (1971), *The Sea Devils*), regularly used hypnosis to gain instant compliance and trust.

Summary

By analysing Eric Roberts' Master against a variety of villain types we have been able to establish a much richer character than is often assumed. More so than any other character in the drama, the Doctor

---

[207] As Lance Parkin observes, this premediated scheming is contrasted with the Doctor's tendency to improvise (Parkin, 'The Galaxy's Most Wanted', p11).

included, the role encapsulates the creative tensions and competing pressures that were at the heart of the enterprise. He is at once camp and macabre, British and American, something borrowed and something new. But by being both the charming and sophisticated trickster of *Terror of the Autons* and the delirious and bitter monster of *The Deadly Assassin*, the danger is that he is reduced to a tribute act, taking his turn at some of the most memorable pick-and-mix features from past eras. In one episode he goes on the same kind of journey that took place across several stories and incarnations. There is too much to process for the viewer to see him as anything other than an archetype.

Newcomers will not have shared the same sense of revulsion and horror as those familiar with Delgado's Master would have done in *The Deadly Assassin*, or the same sense of anticipation that fans experienced when the degenerate Master finally assumed a new body at the end of *The Keeper of Traken*. As such this is not so much the next step in the Master's journey as it is a treatment of an already mythologised character. Unlike the Doctor there are no specific references to past adventures or past lives (at a push we might interpret his Genghis Khan line about the Doctor as a reference to his own past), because his entire history has been conflated into the narrative.

The eighth Doctor continually pulls us out of the closed walls of the drama with his namedropping and confident predictions about the futures of even incidental characters, but the Master repeatedly pulls our focus back in to the core plot. The Doctor defeats him not by undermining his single-minded pursuit of a new body with reminders of his past, but by breaking Grace and Chang Lee's zombified state as nothing but instruments of the Master's present needs. When the

Master dies by tumbling into the Eye of Harmony, in effect he is being consumed by the plot. The character only exists for the story. Any subsequent effort to bring this version of the Master back to life runs the risk of coming across as contrived[208].

---

[208] See the summary of the various attempts in Tribe, Steve, *Doctor Who: A Brief History of Time Lords*, p116.

HOW WELL DO THESE SHOES REALLY FIT?

Jacobs took a variety of approaches when it came to referencing the rich history of **Doctor Who**. He mined its icons, writing them in like Easter eggs, he summarised many of the key points in the opening narration, and he included the seventh Doctor and the Master. A large section of the Leekley bible was taken up with various retellings of classic serials (though Segal has stated that these were not intended as blueprints for a new series, but were merely examples of the kind of adventures the Doctor might face[209]), and Jacobs' script recycles a number of features from one **Doctor Who** story in particular, *The Deadly Assassin*.

Unlike the numerous story proposals in the bible, *The Movie* is a resetting rather than a retelling of the Robert Holmes adventure. There is almost a scattergun approach to the inclusion of visual and story elements, with most of them used in completely different contexts, but the sheer number of similarities can hardly be coincidental:

- The Eye of Harmony is relocated from Gallifrey to the TARDIS, but in both stories the destruction of entire worlds can only be avoided if it is closed.
- The shot of the Master's eyes, relocated from the Matrix to outer space.
- In the Matrix, Goth at one point is disguised as a surgeon and stands over the Doctor with a needle.
- The opening narration, told in both cases by the Doctor.

---

[209] 'The Seven Year Hitch'.

- The fourth Doctor's leather bag in the TARDIS is very similar to the seventh Doctor's.
- Time Lord robes, worn by most characters in *The Deadly Assassin* (including the Doctor) , and by the Master in *The Movie*.
- The Master's mission in both is to be free of a decaying body and to be granted a new cycle of regenerations.
- The Master uses a sidekick in both adventures (Goth and Chang Lee), manipulating them with the promise of power or wealth.
- The design of *The Movie* TARDIS is influenced by the wooden and brass features and the ecclesiastical trappings of the secondary TARDIS console room.
- The Seal of Rassilon is moved from Gallifrey to the TARDIS.
- The torture device used to force a confession from the Doctor resembles that used by the Master to extract the Doctor's lives (in both he is chained with his hands above his head).
- The Doctor wields a gun in an attempt to shoot the president's assassin, but in *The Movie* he turns one on himself.
- The final battle between the Master and the Doctor is relocated from the vault of the Panopticon to the Doctor's TARDIS. In both the Master appears to die from falling into the opened Eye.
- The Doctor turns down an offer to stay, on Gallifrey and Earth respectively.

Despite these extensive associations with the 1976 adventure, there is actually very little to directly tie *The Movie* into the ongoing series.

Even with McCoy's appearance, *The Movie* could be singled out as a tribute or an alternative take rather than a continuation. The Doctor never cites a past televised adventure and no efforts are made to explain the relocation of the Eye of Harmony, the radical redesign of the TARDIS, the Doctor's previous silence on his half-human status, or the fact that he is once again travelling alone. Only the bare minimum of facts are asserted, squeezed economically into the pre-credits narration.

After Segal had failed to secure a follow-up run, it was soon apparent that any eventual new production would be left with the responsibility to either bring *The Movie* into the fold or leave it out in the cold. *The Movie* had simply not done enough to establish itself as an incontestable part of **Doctor Who** lore. It was unrealistic to believe it could work as a standalone, particularly when one of the key features Segal was eager to incorporate, a 1996 equivalent to the Daleks, was scrapped in order to cast an American actor as the main villain[210].

After a brief attempt to keep the flame burning in the hope that a new series would be picked up[211], between 1997 and 2005 *The Movie* received little to no mainstream recognition as part of the continuing adventures of **Doctor Who**[212]. In December 1997 the

---

[210] Jacobs conceded as much when he expressed the desire to introduce such a foe if a series was commissioned (Gillatt, Gary, 'Urban Regeneration', p13).

[211] Most notably in the five-part *Radio Times* eighth Doctor comic strip which ran from June 96 to March 97.

[212] It is important to make a distinction here between acknowledgement and canonisation. The BBC has largely avoided using such a prescriptive term (see Cornell, Paul, 'Canonicity in

officially licensed PC computer game *Destiny of the Doctors* completely ignored the film by implying that the seventh was the most recent incarnation and by casting Antony Ainley as the Master (despite the character channelling Eric Roberts' Master by being attired in Time Lord regalia). The plot of the story, written by Terrance Dicks, centred on the player rescuing all **seven** incarnations of the one 'known only as the Doctor'. Whilst this may have been a rights issue, or to do with the radical redesign of the TARDIS in the movie[213], elsewhere Dicks made clear his antipathy towards the production, ironically and most cuttingly in *The Eight Doctors* (1997). The first book in a range of BBC novels to feature Paul McGann's incarnation includes a particularly harsh assessment of the Doctor's debut story as 'a weird, fantastic adventure, full of improbable events.'[214] The tie-in media continued to present versions of the eighth Doctor that bore little resemblance to *The Movie*, and various interested parties were coming forward proposing a revival as if *The Movie* had never happened[215].

Neither *Scream of the Shalka* (2003) nor *Rose* included a regeneration scene or even a reference to the fact that the Doctor's immediate predecessor was the one played by Paul McGann[216]. Until

---

Doctor Who'), but nevertheless we would expect to see some effort to remind the viewers of the most recent iteration of the character.

[213] *The Movie*'s elaborate set would have been problematic for a game centred on the classic series' TARDISes.

[214] Dicks, Terrance, *The Eight Doctors*, p1.

[215] An exception to this trend is Steven Moffat's 1999 Comic Relief sketch *The Curse of Fatal Death*, in which Rowan Atkinson's Doctor is explicitly the ninth.

[216] Russell T Davies did however give the go-ahead for DWM to include a regeneration scene at the conclusion to the eighth Doctor's

press interest gathered a head of steam, Eccleston's Doctor was never described in-house as the ninth[217]. Davies was not interested in rebooting the series, but neither did he want to be the overseer of a nostalgic or ironic take on the past. His approach to the show's icons was to drip-feed them, so as not to overwhelm the new audience with **Doctor Who**'s extensive mythology[218]. The Daleks are held back until episode six, *Dalek* (2005), and Gallifrey is not mentioned by name until *The Runaway Bride* (2006). The publicity for the revived series, perhaps learning from the mistakes of the past, was focused on what was to come, rather than the history of the series.

It was not until a sketch of the eighth Doctor appeared in the Journal of Impossible Things alongside those of the Doctor's other incarnations in *Human Nature* (2007) that it was firmly established on-screen that the Doctor of *The Movie* was part of a shared (dis)continuity. Whilst the other Doctors were also acknowledged for the first time here, the eighth Doctor uniquely needed such validation, since as a one-off he could still be singled out as part of an alternative history, a dead-end, or aborted timeline to reflect its failure as a backdoor pilot.

The eighth Doctor and his companion Grace were less instrumental in shaping the character of the 21st-century series than were

---

final strip, *The Flood* (DWM #346-353, cover dates August 2004 to March 2005). This version of the strip never made it to print, but is discussed and partially reproduced in Hickman, Clayton, 'Flood Barriers' in the collected edition, *Doctor Who: The Flood*.

[217] Scott, Cavan, 'The Way Back Part 2', DWM #464, p29.

[218] Jon Arnold compares this favourably to *The Movie*'s information-heavy approach (*The Black Archive #1: Rose*, p19).

American series such as **Buffy the Vampire Slayer** (1997-2003), and even shows that had influenced *The Movie* such as **Lois and Clark**. Russell T Davies is certainly not as harsh on *The Movie* as other former producers and script editors[219], but he has always been loath to view the Doctor as half-human, so much so that he came close to including a line that would render the Doctor's experience in 1999 San Francisco as an aberration:

> 'I don't like the half-human thing. He certainly isn't half-human, but it's less interesting to say it simply doesn't count. I always wanted to put in a line where someone says to the Doctor "Are you human?" and the Doctor says "No, but I was once in 1999. It was a 24 hour bunk." Part of the reason I never put that in was it was a bit too self-referential but also I thought I'm spoiling the TV Movie if I do that. In that time, like it or not, the Doctor was half-human. Everything in that story says he was half-human, so you can't not count it. I don't think we can ignore it.'[220]

Davies decided to avoid rewriting the script of *The Movie*, but in his final **Doctor Who** story he signed off in mischievous fashion by introducing a Time Lord who may or may not have been the Doctor's mother. As far as his personal canon is concerned she most certainly is, but her identity is deliberately left open-ended. A number of facts are however well established:

---

[219] He praises it for 'single-handedly [fuelling] a fan industry of novels and comics for a decade' (Davies, Russell T, '**Doctor Who**'s Given Me the Time of My Life').

[220] From the **Toby Hadoke's Who's Round** podcast, quoted in Kistler, Alan, 'Doctor Who: Half Human or All Time Lord?'.

- She is a symbol of both opposition and subservience to Rassilon.
- She is a Time Lord, blessed with the foreknowledge and guile to be able to manipulate a situation like the best of them.
- She can exist both on Gallifrey and on Earth simultaneously.
- She is committed to saving the Doctor.
- She knows the Doctor well enough to take the long way round to ensure that he is carrying a gun when Rassilon arrives on Earth, aware too of his relationship to Wilfred Mott.
- The Doctor know exactly who she is, but is deliberately not letting on[221]. The impression is that this is a revelation we are not supposed to know, akin to the Doctor's name.

Crucially the unnamed Woman makes a decisive intervention, signalling the White Point Star to the Doctor and giving him the alternative play. Her importance to the plot, her knowledge of the Doctor, including his friends and his preference for non-violence, and her sacrificial commitment to his safety all point towards her being a significant person in his life. Speculation on the matter is heavily determined by whether or not the Doctor's half-human status is taken as a given. To maintain *The Movie*'s version of his parentage,

---

[221] The least definitive fact in our list, but a note in the script leaves us in no doubt that the viewers are meant to think he knows who she is. After Wilf asks the Doctor who she was, Davies comments: 'The Doctor just looks. At Wilf. At Sylvia. At Donna, in the distance. Friends, mothers, brides. He's not saying.' Davies, Russell T, *The Writer's Tale*, p641.

the Woman could be interpreted as any notable figure from before or after *The End of Time*, from a regenerated Susan to an aged splinter of Clara Oswald (the latter is a tempting prospect given that her role is completely in keeping with the Impossible Girl's sole raison d'être). In choosing to completely ignore the character by shifting the familial focus to the Doctor's wife (River Song) and her parents (Rory and Amy), Steven Moffat's era made any definitive identification both less possible and less necessary. Indeed, the idea that he might have a human mother is very much back on the table following the Doctor's evasive response to Ashildr's question in *Heaven Sent* (2015):

> 'By your own reasoning, why couldn't the Hybrid be half Time Lord, half human? Tell me, Doctor, I've always wondered. You're a Time Lord, you're a high-born Gallifreyan. Why is it you spend so much time on Earth?'

The other major point of departure for *The Movie* was the design and workings of the TARDIS. A radically different console room had already featured, albeit briefly, in 1976-77, but it was scripted as a 'secondary' alternative to the classic design. The Jules Verne-inspired look of *The Movie*'s TARDIS allowed for the possibility of the internal decor being periodically overhauled. Davies opted for a smaller, more organic theme, as distinct from *The Movie* as it was from the 1963-1989 designs. During Steven Moffat's tenure the TARDIS underwent several alterations with plenty of nods to the original series designs. A number of the stand out features of *The Movie*'s TARDIS also found their way in, from the swivel monitor, analogue sound system, 90s telephone and other retro features, to the 12th Doctor's library.

In terms of how the TARDIS functions, Russell T Davies made no reference to the Eye of Harmony in the cloister room; instead he reimagined the heart of the TARDIS as the time vortex and relocated its power source to inside the central console (*The Parting of the Ways* (2005)). Again, during Steven Moffat's tenure *The Movie* was brought back into the fold, so to speak, with the appearance of the Eye in *Journey to the Centre of the TARDIS* (2013), albeit in a completely revamped form as a literal suspended exploding star, tying *The Movie*'s version more directly to Rassilon's trapped black hole in *The Deadly Assassin*. Moffat's directors have also utilised the visual technique of *The Movie* to film the distorted images of the Doctor and his companion addressing each other through the time rotor (e.g. *The Eleventh Hour* (2010)). Missy's eyes over London in *The Lie of the Land* (2017) are another visual call-back to *The Movie*.

The TARDIS is one of the most discontinuous elements in **Doctor Who**, a point cleverly referenced in *Twice Upon a Time* (2017) when the first Doctor observes that the windows on the 12th Doctor's TARDIS are the wrong size. ('Well, it's all those years of bigger on the inside, you try sucking your tummy in that long,' the 12th Doctor replies.) Originally both a ship and a home, personified by the Doctor in much the same way as he treats Bessie, *The Movie* went much further towards turning the TARDIS into a sentient body capable of independent thinking[222]. The TARDIS was the one aspect of *The Movie* that could effectively signal the Doctor's alien side, and as a result became a constant reminder to the audience that the Doctor's

---

[222] Interestingly, in the reference book consulted by Jacobs, Lofficier noted that 'It has been theorised that a TARDIS was semi-sentient, gifted with rudimentary empathetic qualities' (*The Universal Databank*, p388).

humanness was only partial. Davies, rather than running with the idea that the TARDIS had a life of her own, emphasised instead her almost symbiotic relationship with the Doctor. The ninth and 10th Doctors were more able to control her movements than many of their predecessors. Davies also favoured the companion's journey over the craft. Significantly, Rose and not the TARDIS is Bad Wolf, with the energy of the vortex turning her superhuman. During Moffat's tenure, the TARDIS acquired more of a personality, able to override the Doctor and his companions not simply on the basis of logic or prescient knowledge but also because she could experience human emotions such as jealousy and distrust (see especially *The Doctor's Wife* (2011)). When Clara discovers that the TARDIS does not like her, we are reminded of the Master's opposite suggestion to Chang Lee.

Despite Davies' somewhat conservative dismissal of the Doctor's half-human heritage and the changes made to the TARDIS in *The Movie*, his vision for the show was not that far removed from Segal and Jacobs'. *Rose*, like *The Movie*, takes place in a contemporary setting familiar to its core audience. Both revivals sought to reference the past in such a way as to delight long-term fans without alienating an audience unfamiliar with the show's history. Davies, like Segal, saw the Britishness of the show as its unique selling point, though in his case it is grim, bleak realism that defines this national distinctiveness rather than eccentricity. Tonally Davies' productions share *The Movie*'s balance between the camp and the underplayed:

> 'It was a very important thing to drag it up. It's still fun and light and funny – like **Buffy** was in the first three years, before it went tragic – but it's still a drama. It's not light

entertainment.'[223]

Whilst a full series had been commissioned before a single line had been written, the stakes were just as high as for *The Movie* when it came to proving to the BBC that **Doctor Who** had a future: *Rose* 'had to convince [the BBC] that their faith hadn't been misplaced; that an old, tired, niche, cult sci-fi show could work in the mainstream once again'[224]. In 2005 there is a similar turn towards the Doctor's inner thoughts and emotions that was rarely evidenced in the original run, though this is more a reflection of general trends in TV drama than any overt influence of *The Movie*. More tellingly, the ninth Doctor carries his predecessor's peculiar mix of being relatable and mysterious, approachable and distant, both in and not of the world. As compelling as this list is, it would still be an exaggeration to claim that *The Movie* was a major influence on the show's revival. Some have argued that it demonstrated to the BBC that the show was not completely dead in the water, but it is equally possible that the BBC already knew that much and there was never really a question of the show never returning again.

Russell T Davies' decision to recast the Doctor instead of offering the role to McGann, his aversion to the half-human angle, his preference for a working-class companion and his post-Cool Britannia take on Britishness all contributed towards making *The Movie* feel even more set apart than it already was. Bit by bit however, during Steven Moffat's tenure the movie was slowly brought into the fold[225]. This

---

[223] McClean, Gareth, 'Doctoring the TARDIS'.
[224] Davies, Russell T, et al, *The Shooting Scripts*, p10.
[225] Although this may be in part because of their experience of US TV, there is a greater stylistic affinity between Sax's work in *The Movie*

move was partly a reflection of the fans becoming far less hostile towards *The Movie*, but was also due to the increased success and prominence of the series in America. This appreciation of the eighth Doctor culminated in his return to the screen for the 50th anniversary in 'The Night of the Doctor'.

'The Night of the Doctor'

In what was effectively a prequel to *The Day of the Doctor*, true to form Steven Moffat took the opportunity to reference officially licenced **Doctor Who** tie-in media[226]. Here a number of the eighth Doctor's Big Finish audio companions are saluted by the Doctor as he prepares to drink the Elixir that will regenerate him into a Warrior. The list is selective, but even if copyright issues prevented Moffat from mentioning Grace, the fact that there is no 'and all the rest of you' might suggest a preference for the Big Finish range even over *The Movie*[227]. This is not, however, an attempt to canonise the audio adventures but a means of conveying the length and breadth of the eighth Doctor's adventures in between San Francisco and Karn.

Ohila manipulates the Doctor into accepting that the physician's role is redundant in the Time War by presenting him with the body of Cass, who is beyond help. While Grace and Chang Lee are not named,

---

and that of some directors of post-2010 episodes – especially Nick Hurran, who adopts similar camera techniques (e.g. reflections, unusual angles, jump cuts and speed changes).

[226] C.f. Abslom Daak (*Time Heist* (2014)), the Chelonians (*The Pandorica Opens* (2010)).

[227] Moffat's novelisation of *The Day of the Doctor*, which incorporates the events of 'The Night of the Doctor', extends some of the same consideration to the BBC Books **Eighth Doctor Adventures**, by adding Fitz's name to the list (Moffat, Steven, *The Day of the Doctor*, p18).

there is a certain symmetry between the endings of the eighth Doctor's first and final story. The TARDIS and not the Doctor saves his first associates, and tragically by refusing to step inside the blue box, Cass loses her life. Regardless of the darker presentation of the Doctor in the Big Finish audios, the biggest change to his character comes as a result of his largely ineffectual engagement in the Time War.

The Doctor, appearances aside, is still trying to act as he did with Grace. That thirst for adventure, that free-spirited love of running into danger are evidenced when he answers Cass' 'Is it always like this?' with 'If you're lucky' and urges her to step inside the TARDIS with 'Come on, you'll love it.' He has assuaged any guilt by association by positioning himself outside the Time War as an occasional intervener. It is a ridiculous position to adopt as a Time Lord. We could argue then that the Doctor is desperately trying to be like his old self. This allows him to be given some of Moffat's trademark flippant and cynical lines, which are intended to sound out of place as a sign that the Doctor is out of sorts.

'The Night of the Doctor' revolves around the Doctor's Time Lord status. The revelation of his identity completely alters Cass' perception of him. Crucially, he does not play the half-human card to distance himself from his people. With a Time War raging it is impossible to be both Doctor and Time Lord, and he ultimately chooses to strip himself of the former. His guilt and his realisation of failure lead him to want the transformation to be painful. Instead of being a wounded healer[228], quoting the 'Physician, heal thyself'

---

[228] A description of the nature of Christ's ministry used by the influential Dutch Catholic priest Henri Nouwen (1932-96).

riddle, he demands that he be healed[229]. He believes that paradoxically he can only save others by no longer being a Doctor. Cass could have been saved if he had conformed to her expectations and forced her into the TARDIS at gunpoint without giving her the opportunity to say no. It wasn't her rejection of his offer that killed her, but his inability to force the issue. This physician can only be healed by resigning from his self-appointed position – his evil, his weakness, is his Messiah complex. Whereas the eighth Doctor announced his entrance with a primal 'Who am I?' followed later by a triumphant 'I am the Doctor!' his death is the complete reversal. He reminds Ohila that he calls himself the Doctor, and when he emerges regenerated as a warrior, he can only describe himself in terms of who he isn't – 'Doctor, no more.'

The eighth Doctor is again explicitly likened to Christ, this time through the double whammy of the hypocrisy taunt that in the gospel text Jesus pre-empted from his critics, and in the symbolism of drinking from the cup – a ritual act that calls to mind the last supper, Gethsemane and Jesus' acceptance of death. The eighth Doctor begins his journey in *The Movie* as the resurrected Messiah and ends it in 'The Night of the Doctor' as the crucified Lord. The minisode might owe more to the audios and novels than *The Movie*, but it has been scripted to call to mind just how far the character has changed from his time in San Francisco 1999. Moffat allows that difference to be accounted for either by the Doctor's tie-in adventures, satisfying those who accept some or all of them as valid, or by the Doctor's reactions to the Time War, satisfying those whose engagement is limited to the character's two televised appearances.

---

[229] *Luke* 4.23.

APPENDIX 1: THE RECEPTION OF *THE MOVIE*

These findings are based on a survey conducted between 1 May 2017 and 5 February 2018. 1509 unique entries were received. The results and a more detailed analysis can be found at https://www.altrixbooks.com/2018/10/black-archive-survey-doctor-who-1996.html.

Preconceptions and Context

- Only 32 respondents reported that *The Movie* was their first **Doctor Who** story, suggesting that contrary to the producer's ambitions *The Movie* failed to draw in a significant number of new fans. It's a moot point whether a full series would have been more successful, but our survey found that the 2005 series had to be watched in its entirety before newcomers dipped into previous eras.
- A lack of knowledge about **Doctor Who** and its mythology increased a respondent's confusion over the story.

Questions of Identity

- The nationality of respondents created fewer variables than did their relative familiarity with **Doctor Who**.
- Those of dual citizenship saw less evidence of either Britishness or Americanisation than did solely British or American viewers.
- The Britishness of the Doctor is seen mostly in terms of his character, mannerisms and above all language.
- The American influence on *The Movie* and **Doctor Who** is seen mostly in terms of style, format and above all setting.

- The Britishness of the Doctor was generally more noticeable than signs of Americanisation.

Reactions and Ratings

- The eighth Doctor is by far the most well-regarded character. However, his appearances in 'The Night of the Doctor', the audios and novels are considered more definitive.
- The Master was better received by those already familiar with the character.
- Outside the media furore, the kiss was not seen as a game changer or a big deal. The most memorable scenes were the shooting of the seventh Doctor and the regeneration.
- The regeneration story was rarely considered to be the main plot, with 'the Doctor saves the Earth (again)' the most popular description.

History and Continuity

- Continuity breaks are mostly forgiven, even by those who rate continuity as important. The exception being the Doctor's half-human, half-Time Lord DNA, with only 11% believing that the Doctor is definitely half-human.
- For those who rate continuity as important, the half-human line was more likely to be viewed as the most memorable. For those who saw continuity as of limited or no important, 'These shoes, they fit perfectly' was the line most likely to have had the greatest impact.
- Those whose **Doctor Who** journey began with *The Movie* are less likely to be bothered about continuity matters.

- *The Movie* was not thought to have been particularly influential on the 21st-century series.

APPENDIX 2: AN INTERVIEW WITH MATTHEW JACOBS

Conducted via Skype, 7 June 2017.

Paul Driscoll: One of the major talking points that still rumbles on in relation to [*The Movie*] is the whole British/American debate. Were you specifically instructed to convey the Britishness of the show, and if so, how did you go about it?

Matthew Jacobs: The prime objective was to create a TV show to be broadcast in the States by Fox, co-produced by Universal and the BBC. So inevitably the primary audience was going to be American. The BBC had given up on it, but they were still supporters and so in terms of the writing of it one of the reasons I was hired was because I was British. The previous writers that Universal had were all Americans so Trevor Walton suggested me. He knew my work from **Young Indiana Jones** [1992-93] and from way back in Britain when we went to the National Youth Theatre together. I think he also knew my connections with the Doctor, so I was the first purebred Brit to be connected to the writing of this particular incarnation.

I immediately assumed we would be handing the baton from Sylvester to the new Doctor – right from the beginning there was never any question in my mind about that. The 'Doctor Who Am I' narrative was really a means by which we could introduce the Doctor to a new public. It was a pretty early decision that he would be a British character, but of course the American network also needed to have a homegrown American star. To get an audience that night, it wasn't enough just to rely on this British science fiction show with its relatively small group of followers, of whom only a certain percentage would watch anyway. So that was why the opportunity for the Master was important, as we were able to cast Eric Roberts as the ambulance driver whose body the Master assumes. Also important was the iconic location, the idea of setting it in San Francisco and having the companions come from there.

PD: In an earlier draft of the script the male companion was called Jack. What was the thinking behind changing him to Chang Lee – was that all down to the specific demographics of the Fox audience?

MJ: It was more a case of us deciding to go with Chinatown as a key location. It helped to capture the atmosphere of San Francisco, where you've got a large Pacific presence. The Chinese population there is enormous and we wanted to capture the idea that this community would be bigger by the year 2000. It would bring a richness and a diversity to the ensemble – a Chinese American, a [white] American and a Doctor who is half human.

PD: You've spoken in the past about how much of yourself you bring into your scripts, and your firm belief that even when writing for a franchise like **Doctor Who** it's still about the writer putting his own spin on things based on personal history and experience. It what kind of ways did your own story shape the script, and in particular the character of the Doctor?

MJ: That's obviously a very rich question, and one I've been exploring a lot recently with the documentary[230]. We bring a lot of ourselves to

---

[230] 'Doctor Who Am I', still in production. The documentary follows Jacobs' journey into the world of fan conventions in the USA, having previously avoided them for fear of being 'crucified'. See 'Doctor Who Am I? A Documentary Adventure Through Spacetime and Fandom!'

these fictional characters and to each show that we love. As a writer I inevitably end up bringing my own personal baggage to the table. I'm not afraid of that... it's what marks the film out, gives it a fingerprint and makes it unique. And in my case this quest for identity was a huge part of that. In one scene the Doctor lies down in the grass and has this intimate memory of being with his father and of watching a meteor shower together. I felt an affinity to the Doctor there, in as much as it resonated in terms of my own father's love of art and of the world. The fondness of memory if you like. In the Gary Russell book [*Regeneration*] Segal talks about my deathbed experience with my dad – that was all bullshit. I don't know what Philip Segal was thinking then. I love Philip Segal, we get on very well but I think the history made that all convenient as a story. My dad died when I was in America so I wasn't able to be with him at the end, but I think that idea of regeneration was my way into it.

Also the love of humans is an aspect of the Doctor that I really latch on to. I love that ability he has to step back philosophically and say things like 'Humans, always seeing patterns'. Then there's the idea of being half one thing and half another thing. Most of us go through that to a certain extent simply from being brought up by a mother and a father, but I experienced it more acutely when I was new to America. I felt like I was half-human because I was an alien in a foreign land, so I basically brought that feeling to **Doctor Who** that he is neither one thing nor another, neither alien nor human in a way. But he has a tremendous love for humans. You can see that his relationship with Grace is the best way for him to come back to life. I felt able to attach myself to that emotionally. It helped that I could set the story in San Francisco, as I'd been based there ever since working for George [Lucas]. My family were all there and so it was great that Fox, Segal and the BBC gave me the freedom to say, 'Let's set this in San Francisco.' Even though we ended up shooting it in Canada it was still my adopted home. So all of those things were reflections of my own journey.

PD: One of your early script notes I think sums this up perfectly: the poignant idea that the Doctor can only find himself when he remembers his love for humanity.

MJ: Yes, so it's not just a kiss, he's a deeply romantic character. The eighth Doctor became more of an outsider figure in the Big Finish shows. He gained more edge – which was **good** – becoming involved in horrific wars and things like that. I don't really know much about those shows, but I do know that at the very beginning the eighth Doctor was born into this weird romantic thing that's going on with Grace after she split from her boyfriend. It may be part of the Americanisation where people want to have a human quality to their aliens, like Spock. Yes, that may be part of this and it could even be one of the reasons why the script was greenlit, who knows. It wasn't just my thing either, Geoffrey [Sax] and Phil [Segal] were both also convinced that there should be more humanity to the Doctor as a character.

PD: In one of your early drafts you had the Doctor even see an image of his mother from a bygone age. So he's remembering not only that his father is an alien, but that his mother is from the distant past. I think that's where the 'Who am I?' line originally came in. Once that's all cut out that whole movement happens very quickly and perhaps loses something.

MJ: Yes, and it was going to be connected at the end. But Phil didn't want that and I think he was right at the end of the day. I didn't read any of the previous writers' drafts and so if I accidentally slipped into something that one of the other writers had addressed – fathers, parental, hereditary and the like then he would say, 'No, we don't want to confuse things – go in another direction, Matthew.' He would steer me away from the complex backstory stuff because there was [so] little time between when I was commissioned [and] us making the thing.

PD: Was it true that you were asked to come up with an equivalent to the Daleks, and that you went through the history of the show and settled on the Master?

MJ: Yes – I think I was told we could not use the Daleks because they were the property of Terry Nation and we hadn't done a deal with him, or something like that. So then it was a case of, 'Well, we have to find an alternative.' The choice of the Master was a question of expediency really. We had to cast an American star for Fox. I knew from being a producer and director that to cast a big name as the permanent companion would be really difficult, so it made much more sense to look to Hollywood for the villain of the piece, and the most iconic human-appearing villain in **Doctor Who** was the Master.

PD: Did you consider having a sympathetic side to the Master, or was it always the intention to write him as the absolute embodiment of evil, the antithesis of what the Doctor is?

MJ: I wrote the character very much with Roger Delgado in mind. He had this sort of moustache-twirling theatricality to him. The idea of the Master suddenly finding himself in the body of a snoring ambulance driver is great fun to work with, but the theatrical side of the character really shines through when he borrows an old Time Lord outfit and plays up to it. I always imagined him as a bit of a panto villain. One of the problems with the movie was that it had to do so much. It's no different from any pilot episode. You have to introduce the world, the characters and the way in which the show is going to work. It's also worth bearing in mind that this was the 90s and TV drama was a different animal to what it is now.

So when it came to creating the villain – there wasn't that much space for him. The most interesting part of the film was the relationship between the Doctor and Grace, you know – that story of how the Doctor finds himself. So the beats that you get with the Master are relatively short. He could have been a much richer character if we'd have had more space. But really, he's a lump of goo who morphs into a snake and climbs down someone's throat, I mean how subtle can you get with that? The minute that he wakes up with those green eyes, turns around and strangles his wife, you know he's already a pantomime character.

Eric Roberts embraced all of that. One of the reasons he wanted the role was because he'd studied at RADA and had fond memories of British pantomime and panto villains. The draft script we sent him was full of all these long florid speeches which he absolutely loved. When he arrived on the set and realised we had cut out a lot of that dialogue (quite rightly, because it really did go way over the top) he was understandably upset. He'd learnt all that stuff and was desperate to do it. We ended up having to play along by going back over the script and putting some of those speeches back in. He loved lines like 'life is wasted on the living', a perversion of Oscar Wilde's 'youth is wasted on the young'. These little pearls from the Master were very camp. In fact, Roberts' whole style was very camp. It's the opposite of where the show has gone with the Master since, but it is what it is. The idea was to establish the unique tone of the show. This wasn't going to be **The X-Files**, this wasn't going to be a sort of gritty sci-fi. We wanted to include the capacity for the ridiculous and the comedic. That was totally where we were heading, and one of the ways of achieving that was through the character of the Master.

PD: Do you think the BBC were a bit nervous about that side of things, given that this was exactly where the show had gone in the 80s under John Nathan-Turner?

MJ: I hadn't really followed the show through the 80s, so I didn't really know what they were thinking. I know occasionally Jo Wright would say, 'no, that's exactly why we don't like **Doctor Who**, so don't do that'. So yes, that may well have been part of it.

PD: Nathan-Turner famously had a background in panto and brought some of that camp flair to the table. Reading some of the preproduction discussions, it was almost like the BBC were wanting to go back to the **Doctor Who** of the 60s and 70s and forget the 80s ever happened.

MJ: Yes, maybe. I'm trying to remember the BBC meetings where they were saying things like, 'Do we really need to have a car chase? It doesn't feel right to have a car chase.' I told them, 'It's San Francisco, how can you not have a car chase?' In the end the only car chase that takes place happens on the flat, so it was a case of compromise. But, you know, when something does not take off immediately, people normally look to the writer as to why stuff doesn't work. That's fair enough and the idea that we Americanised **Doctor Who** is a valid criticism. I think it's better that the show came back in 2005 as a very British one. That's how it should have been, but having the eighth Doctor there kept it alive.

PD: Talking again about the American angle, one of the most significant changes was the format of the show, structured around the seven acts with ad breaks.

MJ: Yes, that was very hard.

PD: What sort of issues did it present to you as a writer?

MJ: Well, it was a TV movie so it wasn't officially a series pilot. It was a backdoor pilot which meant that if it was successful then it would get picked up as a series of one hour episodes. The reason it didn't was really a matter of choice between **Sliders** [1995-2000] and **Doctor Who**. It wasn't the ratings. I was familiar with the TV movie format. I'd done quite a few in Britain, all with the BBC actually, so those ones didn't have these commercial breaks, but working on ABC's **Young Indiana Jones** I got used to this business of being there to sell stuff in the commercial breaks. You need to have those cliffhangers before each break. It was almost worth imagining each section, each act as an episode of its own. You could quite easily release the movie on the internet as a series of 14-minute, or 28-minute, shows. That formatting is being followed today online. I was working on a series called **All You Need Is Me**, which is shot here as a subsidiary of Canal Plus and we were doing exactly that; basically making an online feature-length story in 13-minute sections on a full budget.

PD: I guess it does have the advantage of the audience knowing where you are going with it, and where those cliffhangers are going to be, whereas in the current series 45 to 50-minute uninterrupted episodes can have pacing issues – they might for example drag in the middle. It could be argued that the current format allows too much freedom.

MJ: Well, it's a different animal. Basically you run commercial TV so that it's centred around the ads. It's actually a smaller thing now with the rise of digital platforms, but here in the States terrestrial TV is still commercially driven. Your job is to make people watch commercials so you need these high points to keep the tension going and make sure that the audience sticks around for them. It's not a bad thing. In a way movies should be compelling, but it would have been lovely to have the freedom of not having to sell cars.

PD: You mentioned earlier about the short timespan between being commissioned and the show going into production. I understand there were quite a few changes made to the script even after the filming had started, something I'm sure isn't unusual –

MJ: No – all the time.

PD: You've estimated that the finished product was 60 to 70% how you imagined it to be[231], with the rest being not really what you wanted at all. Can you elaborate a little on where you felt the enforced rewrites had a negative impact on the show?

MJ: We ended up with a situation where people got genuinely confused about the mechanics of the story's climax. Originally the millennium star was part of the final act, but they didn't really understand that side of things. They wanted to make it simpler with the Eye of Harmony and to have a big action climax in the Cloister Room. When I wrote it, there wasn't a big fight in the Cloister Room. That entire action sequence was completely different because the Cloister Room is the smallest room in the church. But the TARDIS had been designed to resemble a great cathedral, so basically I had to wing it. This can happen to any writer when you arrive on location or

---

[231] 'The Seven Year Hitch'.

on the set. Also when we did the read-through the day before we were due to film, suddenly everyone was there hearing the script all together for the first time. People came away from that read-through a bit confused. I had to do a second load of rewrites, which we very skilfully kept quiet from the cast. When I finally spoke to Paul he didn't even remember them. So my issues were mainly about the last act because it was an oversimplification. What I didn't like so much, and still don't, is the easy copout of going back in time to bring Grace back to life. That's the element I'd have liked to have found a more graceful solution to.

PD: Originally the characters were to enter the Eye of Harmony and encounter a mirror universe. There are some very interesting and rich ideas in there.

MJ: I ended up writing a movie called 'Mirror', which would have been Francis Coppola's first science fiction movie, in a deal with Disney. It was straight after **Doctor Who** and was based on an original story I'd written as a child. Some of the ideas in that script were in the early drafts of [*The Movie*]. So after they'd been totally washed away I was relieved because I had the chance to do them myself in a separate thing. I didn't care that the show hadn't been picked up, I was on Disney's books to write Coppola's sci-fi film so I was excited about that. I love that idea of the mirror universe and the duality of existence. It's been explored in a couple of films since, with second Earths and various forms of multiverses. They resonate because we live with duality all the time, spending half of our lives asleep.

PD: Coming back to the characterisation of the Doctor, some of the most poignant images of the eighth Doctor are replete with parallels to the Christian messiah. Geoffrey Sax has claimed that the Jesus symbolism was completely accidental and unintended. Was that your recollection, or had you written the Doctor to share certain Christ-like traits and story parallels?

MJ: When I first saw what Geoffrey was doing with it I thought, 'Well, you've really gone down the Jesus route there.' It's inevitable, this comparison of the Doctor to religious figures, because the foundation of almost every prophet is that they come back to life. That's how they establish their credentials. They must be the voice of God because they are too sacred to be killed or to stay dead. Obviously what Geoffrey was going for was *Frankenstein* – we had access to the footage from the movie and we went for that, in a way to puncture that whole resurrection thing. But when he is struggling along the hospital corridor in a shroud, inevitably people draw Christ-like conclusions. Also, because of the way in which he talks about humans I can see why people leap on that. We are talking about a fandom that is worldwide, and I think fans in different countries approach the show in different ways – some like to see the theology behind it, or look at the values that the Doctor is purveying.

PD: This is something that has been explored a lot since Russell T Davies brought the show back. In *Last of the Time Lords* for example, there's a scene in which he virtually comes back from the dead, floating in the air like a transfigured Christ.

MJ: Well you know, what are you going to do? We were going right down that road, a guy gets killed and then he's put in a tomb, and then it's, you know, 'Who moved the stone?' It wasn't like, 'Oh my time's up, I'm going to be turned into a roman candle and come back with a new face.' In [*The Movie*] he gets killed and then **really** gets killed on the operating table. I made a point of stressing the fact that he was dead. The Doctor explains that the regeneration process took too long and that this was the reason his memory was all screwed. It would have been interesting to run with an uncomplicated regeneration, but Americans like that kind of story where somebody doesn't realise they are magical.

PD: We first meet Grace at the opera, watching Puccini's *Madam Butterfly*, and the music and the composer go on to play an important role in the narrative. Originally, though, it was *Turandot* that you referenced in the script. What was the reason for going with *Madam Butterfly* in the end?

MJ: It was just too expensive at the end of the day. We got *Madam Butterfly* instead because it's used all the time and so there are cheaper versions out there. People said, 'Listen Matthew, no-one is going to get the reference anyway,' but of course the **Doctor Who** fans would have. They would like the fact that the Doctor was around when it was written, and they kept that line in of course. I have a particular affection for that opera, and I love the David Hockney design version. It had actually played in San Francisco. I'd seen it with my wife and been blown away. It's interesting – you clutch at whatever reality surrounds you as a writer. When you are writing fantasy the important thing is to always bring truth to the table. The more truth you can bring to fantasy the more powerful the fantasy is.

PD: Otherwise it can all get too gimmicky?

MJ: Well, it becomes clever. That doesn't mean you have to get schmaltzy. You want to start from a place of truth so that you can get into it and really enjoy writing it.

PD: The Doctor's costume has always taken on an iconic significance.

In the eighth Doctor's case he wears a Wild Bill Hickok fancy dress number. Was there any symbolism behind the choice or was it simply a case of the style fitting the character?

MJ: I don't know whether there was symbolism. This was very much the area of Philip Segal. He wanted the Doctor to have the aura of a Byronic, romantic poet. So he wanted the long hair, the velvet and all of that. I didn't really care because this is a big production decision. My feeling was that I wanted the Doctor to choose something that he would recognise. So as he's going through this old pile of costumes he will come across stuff that he recognises – some he likes, others he doesn't. He sees a gun and throws it away, he sees a scarf and instinctively he might go, 'Maybe not.' He's identifying them as he pulls them out, until he sees the frock coat. It's similar to what Hartnell wore, the first incarnation of the Doctor that we know of.

PD: So that scene and the choice of dress is part of that story of the Doctor remembering and rediscovering who he is?

MJ: That's right, so these are little subconscious prompts for him as he's going through that. It's his subconscious, if you like, that's deciding what to wear. And it's nice because he's choosing the outfit from a position of pure instinct, not with a whole bunch of intellectual stuff going on. He's just going through these clothes and he's picking these things out until he likes it. It's all very casual. But the question of how do you dress the Doctor is always a good one. It's interesting to consider how his look is shaped by the era in which the show was made. I mean, right now he looks like a midlife crisis Doctor.

PD: As we've discussed, [*The Movie*] is very much a psychological story – the drama of the Doctor finding himself – but I wonder if there is also a political and social dimension to it, one that you were conscious of when writing the script.

MJ: That's a really good question. I hadn't really reflected on that side of it before. I think one of the best examples is that bit which Geoffrey did so beautifully, when he's cutting around the world on New Year's Eve. Just as we are all getting lost in the climax of the story, we see all of those Earth cities swishing backwards and forwards and those jump cuts around the party attendees. There's sort of a dance going on. I also love the Doctor's relationship with Grace. I think that's the most politically interesting part of the story. She kisses him, but she also says 'No. No, I don't want to come with you.' She's a strong character, a doctor in her own right.

It wasn't until I started exploring things for the 'Doctor Who Am I' documentary that I realised the significance of my father's appearance in *The Gunfighters* [1966][232]. Like Daphne, he plays an American doctor who is visited by **the** Doctor. He was Doc Holliday, albeit with a very bad accent. I hadn't consciously thought about it when I came up with the character's name, but he was Doc Holliday and she was Grace Holloway. It was almost like some 8 or 9-year-old inside me was writing this thing. So there is this weird, magical thing going on. The other kind of social issue that really got submerged was Lee's story, with the Chinese-America[n] gangster element. All of that got completely washed away. Lee's background was much richer in earlier drafts.

---

[232] Anthony Jacobs played Doc Holliday in this **Doctor Who** serial.

BIBLIOGRAPHY

Books

Arnold, Jon, *Rose*. **The Black Archive** #1. Edinburgh, Obverse Books, 2016. ISBN 9781909031371.

Arnold, Jon, *The Eleventh Hour*. **The Black Archive** #11. Edinburgh, Obverse Books, 2018. ISBN 9781909031685.

Arntfield, Michael, and Marcel Danesi, eds, *The Critical Humanities: An Introduction*. New York, Peter Lang Publishing, 2016. ISBN 9781433131943.

> Swart, Joan, 'Psychopaths in Films'.

The Bible, King James Version. 1611. Oxford, Oxford University Press, 1997. ISBN 9780192835253.

Blake, William, *The Marriage of Heaven and Hell*. 1794. Mineola NY, Dover Publications, 1994. ISBN 9780486281223.

Bloom, Harold, ed, *Frankenstein*. **Bloom's Major Literary Characters**. Philadelphia, Chelsea House Publishers, 2004. ISBN 9780791078822.

Bryson, Bill, *Notes from a Small Island*. London, Doubleday, 1995. ISBN 9780385405348.

Butler, David, ed, *Time and Relative Dissertations in Space: Critical Perspectives on Doctor Who*. Manchester, Manchester University Press, 2007. ISBN 9780719076817.

> Butler, David, 'How to Pilot a TARDIS: Audience, Science Fiction and the Fantastic in **Doctor Who**'.

Campbell, Nick, Jude Davies and George McKay, eds, *Issues in*

Americanisation and Culture. Edinburgh, Edinburgh University Press, 2004. ISBN 9780748619436.

Chapman, James, *Inside the TARDIS: The Worlds of Doctor Who*. London, Tauris, 2006. ISBN 9781845111632.

Conan Doyle, Arthur, *The Penguin Complete Sherlock Holmes*. 1887-1927. London, Penguin Books Ltd, 2009. ISBN 9780141040288.

Cook, John R, and Peter Wright, eds, *British Science Fiction Television: A Hitchhiker's Guide*. London, Tauris, 2006. ISBN 9781845110482.

Cull, Nicholas, 'TARDIS at the OK Corral'.

Davies, Russell T, et al, *Doctor Who: The Shooting Scripts*. London, BBC Books, 2005. ISBN 9780563486411.

Davies, Russell T, and Benjamin Cook, *The Writer's Tale: The Final Chapter*. London, BBC Books, 2010. ISBN 9781846078613.

Decker, Kevin, *Who Is Who: The Philosophy of Doctor Who*. London, Tauris, 2013. ISBN 9781780765532.

Dicks, Terrance, *The Eight Doctors*. **Doctor Who: The Eighth Doctor Adventures**. London, BBC Books, 1997. ISBN 9780563405635.

Garcia, Frank, and Mark Philips, *Science Fiction Television Series, 1990-2004: Histories, Casts and Credits for 58 Shows*. Jefferson, McFarland and Co, 2012. ISBN 9780786469178.

Gillatt, Gary, *Doctor Who from A to Z*. London, BBC Worldwide, 1998. ISBN 9780563405894.

Glancy, Mark, *Hollywood and the Americanisation of Britain: From the 1920s to the Present*. London, IB Tauris, 2013. ISBN 9781848854079.

Gray, Scott, and Gary Roberts, *Doctor Who: The Flood*. Tunbridge Wells, Panini, 2007. ISBN 9781905239658.

Hickman, Clayton, 'Flood Barriers'.

Haining, Peter, *The Nine Lives of Doctor Who*. London, Headline Book Publishing, 1999. ISBN 9780747222439.

Hochscherf, Tobias, and James Leggott, eds, *British Science Fiction Film and Television: Critical Essays*. Jefferson NC, McFarland and Co. ISBN 9780786446216.

Wright, Peter, 'Expatriate, Expatriate: *Doctor Who: The Movie* and Commercial Negotiation of a Multiple Text'.

Jacobs, Matthew, *Doctor Who: The Script of the Film*. London, BBC Books, 1996. ISBN 9780563404996.

Lavigne, Carlen, and Heather Marcovitch, eds, *American Remakes of British Television: Transformations and Mistranslations*. Plymouth, Lexington Books, 2011. ISBN 9780739146729.

Steemers, Jeanette, 'British Television in the American Marketplace'.

Hellekson, Karen, 'Memory and the 1996 Remake of **Doctor Who**'.

Layton, David, *The Humanism of Doctor Who*. Jefferson NC, McFarland and Co, 2012. ISBN 9780786466733.

Leitch, Gillian, ed, *Doctor Who in Time and Space: Essays on Themes, Characters, History and Fandom, 1963-2012*. Jefferson NC, McFarland & Co, 2013. ISBN 9780786465491.

Gulyas, Aaron, 'Don't Call it a Comeback'.

Letts, Barry, *Who & Me: The Memoir Of Barry Letts, Doctor Who Producer 1969-1974*. King's Lynn, Fantom Films, 2009. ISBN 9781906263447.

Levine, George, and UC Knoepflmacher, eds, *The Endurance of 'Frankenstein': Essays on Mary Shelley's Novel*. Berkeley, University of California Press, 1979. ISBN 9780520046405.

> Sterrenburg, Lee, 'Mary Shelley's Monster: Politics and Psyche in *Frankenstein*'.

Lewis, Courtlans, and Paula Smithka, eds, *Doctor Who and Philosophy*. Illinois, Open Court, 2010. ISBN 9780812696882.

> Decker, Kevin, 'The Ethics of the Last of the Time Lords'.

Lofficier, Jean-Marc, *Doctor Who: The Universal Databank*, London, Virgin, 1992, ISBN 9780426203704.

Lofficier, Jean-Marc, *The Nth Doctor: An In-Depth Study of the Films That Almost Were*. London, Virgin, 1997. ISBN 9780426204992.

Milton, John, *Paradise Lost*. 1667. London, Penguin Classics, 2003. ISBN 9780140424393.

Moffat, Steven, *The Day of the Doctor*. **Doctor Who: Target Collection**. London, BBC Books, 2018. ISBN 9781785943294.

Nicol, Danny, *Doctor Who: A British Alien?* London, Palgrave Macmillan, 2018. ISBN 9783319658339.

Norton, Charles, *Now on the Big Screen: The Unofficial and Unauthorised Guide to Doctor Who at the Cinema*. Prestatyn, Telos, 2013. ISBN 9781845830847.

Russell, Gary, *Doctor Who: The Novel of the Film*. London, BBC Books,

1996. ISBN 9780563380009.

Segal, Philip, with Gary Russell, *Doctor Who: Regeneration*. London, Harper Collins, 2000. ISBN 9780007105915.

Shelley, Mary, *Frankenstein, Or The Modern Prometheus*. 1818 revised 1831. Oxford World's Classics 1818 text. Oxford, OUP, 1998. ISBN 9780192833662.

Shelley, Percy, *Selected Poems and Prose*. London, Penguin, 2017. ISBN 9780241253069.

Tribe, Steve, *Doctor Who: A Brief History of Time Lords*. New York, Harper Collins, 2017. ISBN 9780062666864.

Periodicals

Doctor Who: The Complete History Volume 47: *Doctor Who (The TV Movie)*, 2017.

Doctor Who Magazine (DWM), Marvel UK, Panini, BBC, 1979-.

Adams, Matt, 'The Best Dressed'. DWM #497, cover date April 2016.

Barnes, Alan, 'The Duelling Master'. *The Essential Doctor Who* #4: *The Master*, cover date March 2015.

Cook, Benjamin, 'New Life for the Old Master'. DWM #514, cover date August 2017.

Gillatt, Gary, 'Renaissance'. DWM #238, cover date May 1996.

Gillatt, Gary, 'Urban Regeneration'. DWM #239, cover date June 1996.

Handcock, Scott, 'Finding an Audience'. DWM #497.

Morris, Jonathan, 'I Came Back to Life Before Your Eyes. I Held Back Death...'. DWM #497.

Parkin, Lance, 'The Galaxy's Most Wanted'. DWM #311, cover date December 2001.

Rigby, Jonathan, 'The Trick or Treat Master'. *The Essential Doctor Who* #4: *The Master*.

Scott, Cavan, 'The Way Back Part 2'. DWM #464, cover date October 2013.

Jonason, Peter, Gregory Webster, David Schmitt, Norman Lii and Laura Crysel, 'The Antihero in Popular Culture: A Life History Theory of the Dark Triad'. *Review of General Psychology* 16(2), 2012.

Leistedt, Samuel, and Paul Linkowski 'Psychopathy and the Cinema: Fact or Fiction?' *Journal of Forensic Sciences* #59, 2014, pp167-74.

Marin, Cristina, 'The Byronic Hero'. *Language and Literature: European Landmarks of Identity* 4 (2), pp81-86.

Paulhus, Delroy, and Kevin Williams, 'The Dark Triad of Personality: Narcissism, Machiavellianism, and Psychopathy'. *Journal of Research in Personality* #36, 2002.

Radio Times, 25 to 31 May 1996.

Ryan, Robert, 'Mary Shelley's Christian Monster'. *The Wordsworth Circle* 19:3, summer 1988.

Television

24. Imagine Entertainment, 20th Century Fox Television, Real Time Productions, Teakwood Lane Productions, 2001-10, 2014.

24: Legacy. Coco/Katz Productions, Imagine Entertainment, 20th

Century Fox Television, Teakwood Lane Productions, 2017.

30 Years in the TARDIS. BBC, 1993.

Babylon 5. Babylonian Productions Ltd, Synthetic Worlds Ltd, 1993-1998.

Batman. 20th Century Fox Television, Greenway Productions, 1966-68.

Battlestar Galactica. Glen A Larson Productions, David Eick Productions, R&D TV, Universal Television, 1978-80, 2003-2009.

Beauty and the Beast. Witt/Thomas Productions, Republic Pictures, 1987-1990.

The Bionic Woman. Harve Bennett Productions, NBC Universal Television, Universal Media Studios, 1976-78, 2007.

Blake's 7. BBC, 1978-1981.

Doctor Who. BBC, 1963-.

> *The Movie*. DVD, 2010.

> > 'The Seven-Year Hitch'. DVD extra.

Jesus of Nazareth. ITC Films, RAI Radiotelevisione Italiana, 1977.

Lois and Clark: The New Adventures of Superman. December 3rd Productions, Gangbuster Films Inc, Roundelay Productions, Warner Bros Television, 1993-97.

Once Upon a Time. Kitsis/Horowitz, ABC Studios, 2011-.

Red Dwarf. Grant Naylor, Baby Cow Productions, 1988-99, 2009, 2012-.

Resistance is Useless. BBC, 1992.

Room 101. BBC, 1994-2007, 2012-.

Episode broadcast 15 April 2002.

The X-Files. Ten Thirteen Productions, 20th Television, 20th Century Fox Television, 1993-2002, 2016-18.

Film

Adamson, Andrew, and Vicky Jensen, dirs, *Shrek*. Dreamworks, 2001.

Burton, Tim, dir, *Batman*. Warner Bros, 1989.

Burton, Tim, dir, *Batman Returns*. Warner Bros, 1992.

Coen, Joel, and Ethan Coen, dirs, *No Country for Old Men*. Miramax Films, 2007.

Demme, Jonathan, dir, *The Silence of the Lambs*. Orion Pictures, 1991.

Herek, Stephen, dir, *Bill and Ted's Excellent Adventure*. Orion Pictures, 1989.

Park, Nick, and Steve Box, dirs, *Wallace and Gromit: The Curse of the Were-Rabbit*. Aardman Animations, 2005.

Schumacher, Joel, dir, *Batman Forever*. Warner Bros, 1995.

Trousdale, Gary, and Kirk Wise, dirs, *Beauty and the Beast*. Disney, 1991.

Whale, James, dir, *Bride of Frankenstein*. Universal Pictures, 1935.

Whale, James, dir, *Frankenstein*. Universal Pictures, 1931.

Yates, David, dir, *Fantastic Beasts and Where to Find Them*. Warner Bros, 2016.

Audio CD

Briggs, Nicholas, *The Light at the End*. **Doctor Who**. Big Finish Productions, 2013.

Gaming

Destiny of the Doctors. Studio Fish, BBC Multimedia, 1997.

Web

'14 British Cultural Quirks and Eccentricities that May Take Visitors by Surprise.' Oxford Royale Academy. https://www.oxford-royale.co.uk/articles/british-cultural-quirks.html. Accessed 29 May 2018.

'Doctor Who Am I? A Documentary Adventure Through Spacetime and Fandom!' Facebook. https://www.facebook.com/doctorwhoami/. Accessed 29 May 2018.

'Icons of England: The 100 Icons as Voted by the Public'. Culture24, 2011. http://www.culture24.org.uk/art362437. Accessed 29 May 2018.

'The 1996 TV Movie'. The Millennium Effect. http://www.millenniumeffect.co.uk/video/index2.html. Accessed 29 May 2018.

Abramovitch, Seth, ''George RR Martin on Writing TV's *Beauty and the Beast*: "It Was Such a Smart Show"'. *The Hollywood Reporter*, 16 March 2017. https://www.hollywoodreporter.com/live-feed/george-r-r-martin-writing-tvs-beauty-beast-was-a-smart-show-986786. Accessed 29 May 2018.

Adams, Stephen, '**Doctor Who** "Had Anti-Thatcher Agenda"'. *The Telegraph*, 14 February 2010. https://www.telegraph.co.uk/culture/tvandradio/doctor-who/7235547/Doctor-Who-had-anti-Thatcher-agenda.html. Accessed 28 May 2018.

Anders, Charlie, '**Doctor Who**'s Steven Moffat: The io9 Interview', io9, 18 May 2010. https://io9.gizmodo.com/5542010/doctor-whos-steven-moffat-the-io9-interview. Accessed 28 May 2018.

Bianculli, David, 'Fox Flick a Who's "Who" of Sci-Fi'. *Daily News*, 14 May 1996. http://cuttingsarchive.org/index.php/Fox_Flick_a_Who%27s_%27 Who%27_of_Sci-Fi. Accessed 4 June 2018.

Berry, Dan, 'Lance Parkin Interview (Part 1)'. *Unreality SF*, 2 June 2008. http://unreality-sf.net/2008/06/02/lance-parkin-interview/. Accessed 29 May 2018.

Clements, Andrew, 'I Think it's all Over'. *The Guardian*, 8 June 2002. https://www.theguardian.com/books/2002/jun/08/artsfeatures. Accessed 29 May 2018.

Cornell, Paul, 'Canonicity in **Doctor Who**'. Paul Cornell: Novelist, Screenwriter, Comics Writer, 10 February 2007. https://www.paulcornell.com/2007/02/canonicity-in-doctor-who/. Accessed 29 May 2018.

Culver, Chris, 'What Makes a Good Villian?' Barnes and Noble Press, 14 August 2014. https://www.barnesandnoble.com/bnpress-blog/what-makes-a-good-villain/. Accessed 29 May 2018.

Davies, Russell T, '**Doctor Who**'s Given Me the Time of My Life'. *The Telegraph*, 18 December 2009.

https://www.telegraph.co.uk/culture/seasonal-culture/6840859/Doctor-Whos-given-me-the-time-of-my-life-Russell-T-Davies-on-leaving-Doctor-Who.html. Accessed 29 May 2018.

Diamond, John, 'Doctor Why?' *The New Statesman*, 31 May 1996. http://cuttingsarchive.org/index.php/Dr_Why%3F. Accessed 29 May 2018.

Doran, Sarah, 'This Fan Theory Has Convinced Us There's a Secret Time Lord Hiding in *Beauty and the Beast*'. *Radio Times*, 8 February 2016. http://www.radiotimes.com/news/2016-08-02/this-fan-theory-has-convinced-us-theres-a-secret-time-lord-hiding-in-beauty-and-the-beast/. Accessed 29 May 2018.

Fordy, Tom, 'What Does **Doctor Who** Say About British Men?' *The Telegraph*, 22 August 2014. https://www.telegraph.co.uk/men/the-filter/11046203/What-does-Doctor-Who-say-about-British-men.html. Accessed 29 May 2018.

Harris, John, 'Cool Britannia: Where Did it All Go Wrong?' *New Statesman*, 1 May 2017. https://www.newstatesman.com/1997/2017/05/cool-britannia-where-did-it-all-go-wrong. Accessed 29 May 2018.

Harrison, Andrew, 'Steven Moffat: "I was the Original Angry **Doctor Who** Fan"'. *The Guardian*, 18 November 2013. https://www.theguardian.com/tv-and-radio/2013/nov/18/steven-moffat-doctor-who-interview. Accessed 29 May 2018.

Heath, Anthony, and Jane Roberts, 'British Identity: Its Sources and Possible Implications for Civic Attitudes and Behaviour'. University of Oxford, 2006.

http://webarchive.nationalarchives.gov.uk/20140207023410/http://www.esrc.ac.uk/my-esrc/grants/RES-148-25-0031/outputs/Read/5dfb4628-3a97-44d5-9c05-d9df56f4fd6d. Accessed 29 May 2018.

Horowitz, Anthony, 'Sherlock v Moriarty: Perfect Foes'. *The Telegraph*, 18 October 2014. https://www.telegraph.co.uk/culture/books/11167631/Sherlock-v-Moriarty-perfect-foes.html. Accessed 29 May 2018.

Hughes, Mike, '"Blue" Cop Sags Tonight'. *Lansing State Journal*, 14 May 1996. http://cuttingsarchive.org/index.php/The_original_series_was_terribly_British. Accessed 29 May 2018.

Kistler, Alan, 'Doctor Who: Half Human or All Time Lord?' Tor.com, 14 December 2015. https://www.tor.com/2015/12/14/doctor-who-half-human-or-all-time-lord/. Accessed 29 May 2018.

Lambess, Neil, 'A State of Temporal Grace'. *Time/Space Visualiser* #46, August 1997. http://doctorwho.org.nz/archive/tsv48/temporalgrace.html. Accessed 29 May 2018.

Leane, Rob, 'Doctor Who Film: Steven Moffat "Happy", But Must Not "Damage the Series"'. *Den of Geek*, 23 April 2015. http://www.denofgeek.com/tv/doctor-who-movie/35124/doctor-who-film-steven-moffat-happy-but-must-not-damage-the-series. Accessed 28 May 2018.

Martin, Daniel, 'Who Do We Think We Are? **Doctor Who**'s Britain'. BFI, 2014. http://www.bfi.org.uk/features/doctorwho/. Accessed 28 May 2018.

McEwan, Cameron, 'Steven Moffat Reveals Why He Didn't Bring Eric Roberts Back to **Doctor Who** as the Master'. *Digital Spy*, 9 November 2017. http://www.digitalspy.com/tv/doctor-who/news/a842592/doctor-who-master-series-10-steven-moffat-eric-roberts-return/. Accessed 29 May 2018.

McClean, Gareth, 'Doctoring the TARDIS'. *The Guardian*, 7 March 2005. https://www.theguardian.com/media/2005/mar/07/mondaymedia section. Accessed 29 May 2018.

Minkel, Elisabeth, 'The Global Force of **Doctor Who**'. *The New Statesman*, 20 August 2014. https://www.newstatesman.com/culture/2014/08/global-force-doctor-who-what-does-britain-s-biggest-cultural-export-tell-world. Accessed 28 May 2018.

Moran, Caitlin, 'Torrid in the TARDIS'. *The Times*, 31 March 2007. https://cuttingsarchive.org/index.php/Torrid_in_the_Tardis. Accessed 29 May 2018.

Mulkern, Patrick, 'Steven Moffat Reveals (Almost) All about the Doctor Who Christmas Special'. *Radio Times*, 7 December 2016. https://www.radiotimes.com/news/2016-12-07/steven-moffat-reveals-almost-all-about-the-doctor-who-christmas-special/. Accessed 11 June 2018.

Murashev, Dmitry, 'DM's Opera Site'. http://www.murashev.com/opera/. Accessed 4 June 2018.

Narval Media, Birkbeck College and Media Consulting Group, 'Stories We Tell Ourselves: The Cultural Impact of UK Film, 1946-2006'. BFI, 2006. Available at http://www.bfi.org.uk/about-bfi/policy-strategy/consultations-publications/publications-archive. Accessed 29 May 2018.

Newman, Kim, '**Doctor Who** Has Been Exterminated'. *The Independent*, 29 May 1996. http://cuttingsarchive.org/index.php/Dr_Who_has_been_extermin ated. Accessed 4 June 2018.

Northern Alliance, Ipsos MediaCT, 'Opening Our Eyes: How Film Contributes to the Culture of the UK'. BFI, 2011. http://www.bfi.org.uk/about-bfi/policy-strategy/opening-our-eyes-how-film-contributes-culture-uk. Accessed 29 May 2018.

Plauche, Geoffrey, 'American vs British Science Fiction'. *The Libertarian Standard*, 1 May 2010. http://libertarianstandard.com/2010/05/01/american-vs-british-science-fiction/. Accessed 29 May 2018.

Rosa, Joseph, 'Wild Bill Hickok: Pistoleer, Peace Officer and Folk Hero'. HistoryNet. http://www.historynet.com/wild-bill-hickok-pistoleer-peace-officer-and-folk-hero.htm. Accessed 29 May 2018.

Sillito, David, 'Rock 'n' Roll PM: Blair's Cultural Legacy'. BBC News, 10 May 2007. http://news.bbc.co.uk/1/hi/uk_politics/6557625.stm. Accessed 29 May 2018.

Sykes, Tom, 'The Best Eccentrics Are British, Obviously'. *The Daily Beast*, 4 June 2016. https://www.thedailybeast.com/the-best-eccentric-aristocrats-are-british-obviously. Accessed 29 May 2018.

Tilley, Doug, and Liam O'Donnell, 'The Eric Roberts is the Fucking Man Podcast'. Episode 62, 12 November 2017. http://www.ericrobertsistheman.com/episode-62-live-cinepocalypse-film-festival-eric-roberts/. Accessed 29 May 2018.

BIOGRAPHY

Paul Driscoll is an author, editor and publisher based in Leigh in Greater Manchester, UK. He is a proud dad to six children, aged from 22 to three. In 2015 he gave up a long-term career in the charity and voluntary sector to concentrate on writing, editorial work and selling cult film and television merchandise. In 2018 he co-founded Altrix books (http://www.altrixbooks.com) with fellow **Black Archive** writer, Kara Dennison. This is his second **Black Archive** book, following on from *The God Complex*, **Black Archive** #9. Other works include the **Seasons of War** charity novel *Gallifrey* (with Kara Dennison, Altrix Books, 2018), short stories in *A Clockwork Iris*, (Obverse Books, 2017), *Nine Lives* (Red Ted Books, 2017), *Time Shadows: Second Nature* (Pseudoscope Publishing, 2018), *Children in Time* (kOzmic press, 2018) and various essays in the **You and Who** series of books, most recently *You and 42: The Hitchhikers Guide to Douglas Adams* (Who Dares Publishing, 2018).

Coming Soon